CH♥COLATE
ROSES

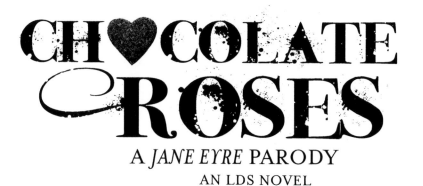

CH♥COLATE ROSES

A *JANE EYRE* PARODY

AN LDS NOVEL

JOAN SOWARDS

To my girls,
Tasanee, Kristy, and Lizette.

Chapter quotes from *Jane Eyre: An Autobiography,* by Charlotte Bronte

Walnut Springs Press, LLC
110 South 800 West
Brigham City, Utah 84302
http://walnutspringspress.blogspot.com

ISBN: 978-1-935217-62-6

ACKNOWLEDGMENTS

My love and appreciation to Kerry Blair—I am only one of the hundreds of writers she has cheered on, forever I give my gratitude; and to Linda Prince and Amy Orton for believing in Chocolate Roses.

Thank you to Gordon Terpening, owner of Chocolàte in Bisbee, Arizona, for the tour of his chocolate shop. His is one of only about 30 shops in the United States that make their chocolate from scratch by grinding the cacao bean. Visit Chocolàte at 134 Tombstone Canyon Road the next time you are in that unique town. The store's website is spiritedchocolate.com

Last but not least, thank you to Tasanee, Kristy, Joanne, Micaela, LeeAnne, Celeste, and Marilyn, for reading my first draft and encouraging me to go forward in spite of it; and to the members of the American Night Writers Association for their help and support. And to Dennis, the love of my life—thank you for cheering me on.

PROLOGUE

In high school, my English teacher required us to read Charlotte Bronte's *Jane Eyre*. I related to poor Jane not because her deceased uncle's family abused her—because my Aunt Lucy, whom my sister Kylee and I went to live with after our parents' fatal car accident, treated us royally—but because as an orphan, Jane had to be strong and find her own place in the world. I wanted more than anything to find my own niche in life . . . and my own Mr. Rochester.

Janie Rose Whitaker

ONE

I had not intended to love him; the reader knows I had wrought hard to extirpate from my soul the germs of love there detected; and now, at the first renewed view of him, they spontaneously revived, great and strong! He made me love him without looking at me.

At 9:00 AM every Tuesday, Roger Wentworth walks into my chocolate shop. There is nothing unusual about his entrance. He walks in just like anybody else. I can predict his order even before he parts those perfectly shaped lips of his: one chocolate rose to be sent to Eden's Garden—an upscale psychiatric hospital—and one small chocolate figure to take with him.

He hardly looks my way as I slip the rose and tissue into a box bearing the store's label. As the artist, I sign the box with my name—Janie.

Tuesday is our slowest day of the week. Even though I arrive at the shop at 7:00 AM, put on my cute apron bearing the Chocolate Art Forever logo, and set to work, at 8:56 something awakens in me. Blood pumps wildly through my veins, causing my heartbeat to knock loudly in my ears. My hands shake. I try not to glance toward the door, but sure enough, at 9:00 sharp, the bell over the door chimes and in walks Mr. Gorgeous. My knees suddenly go weak.

In spite of the faraway look of sadness in his dark blue eyes, he is always dressed like he just stepped out of a Nordstrom catalog, wearing a suit and tie and colored shirt, with his dark brown hair perfectly combed. He walks up to the counter like a man with a purpose and looks over the prices—as if he doesn't already have them memorized—posted above my specially combed Tuesday hairdo (dark and straight to the shoulders as always). He hardly looks at me, so I've grown to admire his profile—a lot. Then he gives me his order. Today, it is the usual Signature chocolate rose and a two-inch-high laughing clown. Last week he chose a swan.

Mr. Wentworth never signs a card, so I have no clue what relationship the recipient is to him. But since she has a dated first name, I imagine Winnie Wentworth as an elderly lady with white hair, hot-rodding around in wheelchair, completely out of her mind.

I wrap the small figure carefully (as carefully as one can with trembling hands) and he gives me his debit card. I rub my thumb over the raised letters printed there—Roger Wentworth III—and stifle a sigh as I swipe the card, knowing our hands almost touched. Sappy, huh?

I hand him his debit card, then say as professionally as possible, "Thank you, Mr. Wentworth. We'll send the rose immediately."

He smiles politely without ever really seeing me, takes the tiny gift box, and heads toward the door. The bell chimes again as the door closes behind him.

So, that's the way it goes every week. Hardly any variation. Yep, it's that predictable. And if you guessed that I've fallen in love with Roger, you're right, I have. Okay, I'm infatuated, at the very least. Not that I have much hope anything will ever come of it. At first I resisted falling for him, but he won me over with the way he walks, his voice, the color of his blue eyes, even the way he pulls the wallet from his back pocket and flips out his debit card. He totally owns my heart, without even trying.

Once in a while, he will smile, which sets my heart a-thumping. Sometimes he will say, "Have a nice day," before he turns and walks out. Seeing Roger every Tuesday *makes* my day, so why should he tell me to have a nice one? Oh, how I wish he would stay and talk, if only for half a minute.

I've imagined the way our relationship will blossom. After lingering at the counter that extra half minute for a few weeks, he will ask me for my phone number. I've imagined sitting beside him in his Lexus, holding hands as we walk around the temple, and even our first kiss.

But none of this has happened. He still treats me as if I'm merely the counter girl, week after week.

I know. I'm hopeless. Someday I will lift the extended counter separating me from the public, walk out there, and put out my hand. "Hi, I'm Janie," I'll say. "Shall we sit and get to know each other?" I'll point to one of our four parlor tables with matching chairs, and he'll gladly sit. We'll talk, and then he will ask me out to dinner.

Such fantasy. At the rate this relationship is going now, it will never happen.

So, you ask, who is this hopeless person? My name is Janie Rose Whitaker. My sister Kylee and I own Chocolate Art Forever, a small shop in downtown Tempe, Arizona. Kylee is the brains of our outfit—accountant, advertiser, store manager—and I am the talent. I wish I could also say I'm the beauty, but I'll have to settle for talent. Blame it on the chocolate.

I am single, of course, or I wouldn't be gawking over Roger Wentworth every Tuesday morning. And I am twenty-seven, so I'm still categorized as a "young adult" in our Mormon culture.

Besides Kylee and me, six people work in our shop. There's Carmen, who comes in every morning at 5:00 and looks after the chocolate-making cycle (what would I do without her?). Then there's Carmen's teenage daughter Cricket, who has that name because she has an eternal, random hiccupping problem. There's Linc, our deliveryman, and Willa (named after Willa Cather), who is our jack-of-all-adventures afternoon help. Our shop is open Friday and Saturday evenings to catch the downtown Tempe nightlife, and Tessa and Frank Ship, a semi-retired couple, take over at 5:00 PM.

As you can see, each person on my staff is unique and important. Oops! I've dumped a lot of information on you. Can you remember it all? You'd better because there is a quiz later (really).

TWO

"For one thing, I have no father or mother, brothers . . ."
"You have a kind aunt."

One day, after Roger Wentworth left the shop and our morning rush was over, I went to work in the kitchen as usual. Carmen finished dipping truffles and went home for the day. October had arrived, so we were filling molds with fall and Halloween themes.

I heard the back door of the shop swing open. "Hi, Janie!" Kylee called. She bounced in, full of enthusiasm and energy, her shoulder-length brown curls *boing*-ing as she walked, like a high school cheerleader's. Well, she's always been *my* cheerleader and confidante.

"All going well?" she asked as she grabbed a clean Chocolate Art Forever apron and entered the office. (Our store has an office, kitchen, and shop. Simple.)

"Just fine. We've had more than the usual number of customers already this morning."

"And the reticent Mr. Wentworth?" she asked, tying the apron.

I didn't miss the glint in her eye. You see, she knew about my secret infatuation. So did everyone in the shop, so I guess it really wasn't a secret.

I stood in the office doorway. "He just left."

"Did you get any information from him?"

On Tuesdays, the first topic every employee in the shop asked about was Roger Wentworth.

"No," I said. "I didn't try."

"What did he order? Another swan?"

"No. A clown."

"He hasn't chosen that before." She pulled that week's folder of bills from the file and started thumbing through them.

Even Kylee, who is happily married to big-guy Boy Scouter and high school PE coach Jim Arnold, and Carmen, who is a widow and about fifty years old, couldn't resist peeking when the attractive Mr. Wentworth came in the shop. No other customer created as much discussion in our shop as he did.

The back door opened again and in walked Linc, our delivery person. "Hi, Kylee," I heard him say. "How are your bambinos today?"

"Fine. They're all fine." She didn't sound interested in chatting, probably because she was already submerged in paperwork.

Linc walked into the kitchen. "You set?" he asked me in his ghetto lilt.

I glanced at him. His shoulder-length hair was braided in cornrows—a new style for him. "Well, look at you. Have you been to the beauty parlor?"

"Nah." He grinned. "The girl next door wanted to practice on me last night. You like?"

"The girl next door?" I said with a deliberate hint of teasing. "Is she cute?"

As he turned around to give me a view of the back of his hair, the braids flipped with him. "She's a hottie but a religious freak."

I chuckled. In Linc's mind, someone who occasionally took the Lord's name in vain was religious. I love that kid like a brother but I don't push the Church on anyone. I only speak in generalities on certain points if the subject lends itself.

"Are the deliveries ready?" He tossed the truck keys in the air and caught them.

"All ready." I motioned toward the boxes stacked on the counter. "Except for this rose going to Eden's Garden. Give me a minute. I still have to tie the bow."

Linc leaned his slight frame on the counter. "That place gives me the creeps."

"What do you mean?" I glanced up from cutting pink ribbon.

"Nothin'. It has them beautiful gardens and all, but going inside is jus' eerie. I leave the box with the old chica at the front desk and practically run out. Can't relax at all 'til I'm outta there."

"Well," I said, re-tucking the tissue and closing the pink and brown box. "I'm sure Winnie appreciates your bravery." I added my signature.

"Who is Winnie, anyway? A patient?"

"Or an employee. I don't know, and it's none of our business."

"Sure it is," Linc said. "This is our business, so it's our business."

"May I remind you that our code of conduct is professionalism? See my nose?" I pointed to the center attraction of my face. "It's short for a reason."

"Yes, and it's lovely, too," he said with mock flattery. "Next time that Wentworth dude walks in, just say, 'Oh, is Winnie an employee there?' He'll say yes or no, and then we'll know."

"Or he will tell me it is none of my business."

"And then we'll know." He raised an eyebrow. "Why wouldn't he say—unless she's one of the nuts in that nuthouse?"

"Linc! Have some respect for the mentally ill. I hope you don't say those things when you're at the hospital."

"You know ol' Linc has more class than that, but just remember, everybody is a freak to somebody."

"Yeah, look at you!" I motioned toward his braids.

He grinned as I handed him the box.

"Now get on your way," I urged. "If you're feeling brave, you can flirt the receptionist into telling you about Winnie."

Linc shuddered, shook his head, and left with the deliveries.

Linc's full name is Lincoln Rockefeller Gates. Impressed? Don't be. There's no relation to the big guys. He's short for his twenty-one years. We discovered him in our shop practically drooling on the glass over a chocolate bunny, of all things. So, in order to keep our glass clean—and besides, he was so cute and had "Will Work for Chocolate" written across his forehead in invisible ink—and since we were desperate for a driver, I offered him a job. Plus, he is half Hispanic and half black, so he adds a little ethnic diversity to our shop.

The morning passed quickly. Though business practically squeals to a halt during the hour before noon, the store's door chime was ringing almost constantly by 11:30. Kylee and I boxed orders as quickly as we could.

At noon, without warning, in walked Roger Wentworth. I thought I was dreaming, for the man often appears in my dreams. He sauntered over to the glass showcase and waited.

The woman I was waiting on recited a long list of items she wanted, including two pounds of pecan fudge. I wished she had a built-in "pause" button so I could wait on Roger first.

Kylee glanced at me knowingly. "I'll be right with you," she said to Roger.

"No hurry." He slid his hands into his pocket and leaned against the glass case.

Kylee finished with her customer and handed the woman a bag bearing the Chocolate Art Forever logo. "Thank you for stopping in," Kylee said warmly, and then turned to Roger. "How may I help you?"

"I need something for an administrative assistant, a woman. It's her birthday," he explained. "How about this happy-birthday balloon bouquet?" He pointed to the sign with the price clearly marked.

"A good choice," Kylee said a bit too enthusiastically. After getting a box and some pink tissue, she opened the case and carefully removed the chocolate balloon bouquet.

Blood pounded in my ears. Roger Wentworth stood close enough that I could have reached out and touched him. His eyes were a deeper blue than ever, and his dark chocolate hair called out for me to run my fingers through it. And those lips!—well, maybe I shouldn't go there. The worry lines on his brow and a scar under his left ear were the only flaws on that beautiful man, beside the eternal sadness in his eyes.

I don't know why I said it. "Your order for Winnie Wentworth has been sent out already." I probably sounded like a ten-year-old girl trying to act older than her age.

Roger glanced up briefly. "Thanks," he said, studying my face a moment as if trying to remember if we had met. I don't think he came up with any memory of me, because he only said goodbye, turned, and walked out of the store.

"Have a nice day!" I called after him, but he must not have heard me.

THREE

It is in vain to say human beings ought to be satisfied with tranquility: they must have action; and they will make it if they cannot find it.

I had been a member of singles wards for eight years. I attended strictly for spiritual enlightenment. Believe that? I didn't think so. The truth is I came to that conclusion because none of the men there paid any attention to me. I don't know why, because I'm not bad looking.

I could've blamed my singleness on the chocolate I wear on my hips. *Sigh.* My philosophy is that if God wanted us to be skinny, He wouldn't have created chocolate. I'm sure chocolate is the favorite food in heaven.

It's hard to be a chocolatier and not have a nibble once in a while. Okay, I admit I do more than nibble, and it's *way* more often than once in a while. You can't blame me. Surely you've heard the saying, "There is a thin person inside of me screaming to get out, but I keep her sedated with chocolate." I could have written that. Another of my favorites is, "When the going gets tough, eat chocolate."

I've worked hard to perfect my recipes. If some of those men in the singles ward would've sampled my talents, they would've agreed and asked me out. The way to a man's heart is through his stomach, you know, especially if what goes through his stomach is chocolate.

At Chocolate Art Forever, our specialty is artwork in chocolate. We carry *art masterpieces* in chocolate. Of course, we still carry fudge and assortments sold by the pound for all you non-artistic chocolate appreciators.

You may think twenty-seven is young to be a shop owner, but Kylee's and my parents and younger brother died in a fatal car accident when we were young. Our parents left us a sizeable inheritance, and after we graduated from college, we decided to use our trust fund to set up shop—literally.

Losing our parents was the hardest time in my life. If it wasn't for Kylee, I don't think I would have made it. She and I went to live in Wickenburg with our eccentric aunt Lucy. She is retired now and somewhat of a philanthropist, but by profession, she is an eating disorder therapist. She's a wonderful person who spends every minute saving the world in one way or another, so we don't see much of her.

When we lived with Aunt Lucy, she left us much to ourselves—to fend for our own meals and upbringing—but took us to church every Sunday, where she got pumped up for the week by teaching the Gospel Doctrine class. I think I became independent too young, you know, having to rely on myself. I never made close friends other than Kylee.

Our ward, especially our attentive Primary teachers and Young Women leaders, became our family. If it hadn't been for a certain boy named Trevin Worliss, a self-appointed thorn in my side, that small town would've been the perfect place for anyone to grow up in. That kid continually found a way to push the thorn deeper. For instance, the day I got my braces, he called me Santa Fe (the name of the railroad that ran through our tiny town), and the name stuck. When I go back to Wickenburg to visit Aunt Lucy, I steer clear of Trevin.

But now I'm away from there and have found my niche in life as a chocolatier.

We make most of our chocolate from scratch. The process of preparing chocolate is lengthy and involved, so I'm giving you the streamlined version. (If you aren't interested, then skip to the next paragraph, but who isn't interested in chocolate? Nobody I know.) First we roast the cocoa bean, then crack it, then winnow it—blow off the husks. Next, we grind the nibs and sugar into cocoa liqueur—don't worry, nobody gets drunk—then conch and refine it. Last of all, we temper the chocolate. We have machines for each of these steps, thank goodness, because otherwise it is a lot of work.

I burned out attending singles wards, so I started going to a family ward. I returned to the mainstream Mormon way of Sunday worship because, number 1, I missed Cheerios on the pews and finding crayons in the hymnbook holders; and number 2, I missed crying babies during the sacrament. Number 3 has already been hashed-out in the above paragraphs. Honestly, what I missed most was the whole spectrum of Church membership, from the newborn baby to the practically deaf elderly brother wearing headphones on the front row, and you don't find that in a singles ward. It's just too bad that in most family wards, there are hardly any single men under the age of seventy.

Back to my chocolate-enriched hips and then I won't mention them again, I promise. You know that scene in the beginning of *Peter Pan* when Tinkerbelle stands on a hand mirror in

Wendy's bedroom? Tink looks down at her reflection, puts her hands on her hips, and raises her hands to see how wide they are. Proportionally, Tinkerbelle would look like me. Get it? Slender to the waist, but a little ample in the behind.

My only consolation is that the world loves Tinkerbelle. Aunt Lucy, who is an old maid (ironic, huh?), reminds me that "A man isn't looking for a skinny wife. He is looking for a happy wife." When I quote it to myself, I naturally smile and laugh all jolly-like. What she wants me to get from it, I suspect, is to be cheerful and show off my $4000 worth of orthodontic work.

I used to smile at all those men at the singles ward, but what good did it do me? I still have hips, and being single into one's late twenties isn't the end of the world.

I haven't been totally truthful about my wallflower status. There was one guy in my life named John, and I met him at the pet food store. He was buying a seven-ounce can of fish food, while I was there for one hundred pounds of dog food. Of course, he thought that meant we had a lot in common.

John stood six foot three and resembled a big teddy bear. He was the only guy I had dated more than once in several years. After our once-a-month date, I'd tell myself I shouldn't be dating nonmembers and resolve to tell him no when he called again, but by the time another month rolled around, I'd feel starved for male attention. Even the lame attention John gave me was better than none. He was more like a brother instead of a boyfriend, and at the doorstep, it was always a handshake instead of a kiss, which was fine with me. He claimed to be a diehard Baptist—meaning not the converting type—had a Southern accent, and made me laugh with his goldfish imitation.

John stopped in the shop once in a while. The first time he

came in, he mistook Kylee for me and asked her out. Can you hear me snickering? That's how well he knew me. (Kylee is four years older than me and is married with three kids.) John did all the talking on our dates. He was a professional student, religious, laidback, over thirty years old, and not in any kind of hurry to find a job, or a wife. Maybe his inability to make commitments made it easy for him to keep calling me. I was safe and unmarriageable because I'd only marry a Latter-day Saint, so we had a go-nowhere relationship. *Too* tranquil if you ask me, but nobody did.

Later the same day, after Roger came in unexpectedly and bought the balloon bouquet, I finished waiting on a customer and turned around to find Kylee standing in the doorway to the kitchen. She had this pained look on her face that I've come to know is her this-is-hard-for-me-to-say look. "I won't be in until noon tomorrow. I've already arranged with Carmen to stay until I get here."

"Are you going somewhere fun without me?"

"No, just a doctor's appointment."

"Is everything all right?" I asked.

"No," she said with short sigh. "Just the usual." She went into the office and I knew not to follow. Kylee has lamented ever since Jaxlynn, her now six-year-old, graduated out of diapers, that she hasn't had another child. Doctors have suggested everything from vitamins to herbs, and exercise to relaxation, to remedy the undiagnosed problem.

"Quit working," one specialist ordered. "You are under too much stress." That lasted about three days before I found Kylee back in the shop. In order to keep her mind off her empty arms, she *has* to come into the shop. I keep telling her that she needs to sit and relax with a box of chocolate truffles, but she doesn't buy my theory, claiming they only make her fat.

Anyone outside the Mormon Church—I mean, The Church of Jesus Christ of Latter-day Saints—would think three children made up a BIG family. But inside the Church three is small. Besides, Kylee has this constant longing and a nagging feeling there is another child waiting to join her family.

I heard the back door slam and Linc's familiar whistle, accompanied by rhythmic clapping.

"So, did you flirt with her?" I asked, settling on the stool behind the counter as a customer left the shop.

"Who?" He had a look of innocence on his face. (I've noticed the same feigned look when he has a yummy secret.) He stopped clapping.

"Eden's Garden's receptionist." I resisted rolling my eyes.

"Oh!" He laughed and relaxed. "The nurse was a beauty—wide as a door and old enough to be my granny." He grabbed a broom and waltzed with it to the open extended counter, then out to the public side of the shop. He and his stick partner made a few more twirls before he started sweeping the concrete floor under the parlor tables and chairs.

"Well? Did you ask?" Was he really intent on getting the job done before another customer came in, or just ignoring me?

He stopped in mid-sweep. "Yep. Their privacy policy won't let them give out that kind of information."

"Really?" I huffed. "You get checked in and immediately become top secret."

"Something like that. But I saw Granny write a room number on the card." He straightened up the chairs.

I envisioned a sturdy-built, white-haired nurse wearing a sterile cap and uniform, writing with a chubby hand on one of our Chocolate Art Forever cards. "Even offices have numbers." I said.

"And then she turned to an assistant—who, compared to Granny, was actually cute, but I didn't get a chance to show her how charming I was—and said, 'Please deliver this to room 147.'"

"Hmm."

"Hmm, is right," he continued. "If Ms. Wentworth was an employee, she would have said—"

"Deliver this to Winnie."

Now I knew, or at least felt pretty certain, that Winnie Wentworth was a patient at the psychiatric hospital. I didn't know her relationship to Roger. That, and the reason behind his sad eyes, was yet to be discovered.

FOUR

I am no bird; and no net ensnares me; I am a free human being with an independent will.

I rent a small apartment at Taylor Palms across the street from the Mesa Temple. Driving to my shop in downtown Tempe can take a while in rush-hour traffic, but seeing the temple from my home compensates for the long drive. In fact, the sight of the temple makes me so happy that it's almost like daily therapy. I love the atmosphere that centers around the temple during the Easter Pageant and the Christmas lights, too, and living in the middle of all the excitement.

I usually refer to my place as a "cottage" because it's tiny and it's free-standing—and because "cottage" sounds homier than "apartment." Don't you agree? My cottage must have been built in the Ice Age, since it is sadly crumbling and has been patched, mended, and plastered over more times than Elizabeth Taylor's face. Thus, I'm sure, the name.

I live alone with my dog, Florentine. She is the reason I buy

100 pounds of dog food at a time. Flo is a chocolate-colored Great Dane (the only color appropriate for a chocolatier), and you can imagine how she gets to feeling pretty cooped up in our tiny three-room cottage. When I met her as a pup, I knew she was for me, being chocolate and all. The breeder said her dark color is a recessive gene and very rare. Flo weighs 120 pounds and Aunt Lucy accuses me of putting Miracle-Gro in her water dish. The truth is, I've given up on water dishes and just fill the bathtub.

Some people think I'm crazy for keeping such a big dog in such a small apartment. I know, Great Danes need ranch-sized spaces to roam. We have a cinderblock-enclosed backyard that isn't ranch sized—it's barely 10 by 10 feet square—that she romps in during the day when I'm at work. She spends her time barking at pedestrians, who probably don't realize all that ferociousness is only a call for someone to come play.

Most evenings after sunset, Flo and I go for our usual walk around the temple. (Well, she really drags me. I just go with the Flo. Get it?) We don't walk on the grounds, just the surrounding sidewalk, so don't worry, those lovely flowers are safe. Flo loves to dress up to go out, so she brings me her yellow bandana as my cue that she's anxious to leave. I tie it around her neck before we head out the door.

One evening, as Flo and I rounded the corner of Kimball and LeSueur streets, a man approached from the rear. "I believe you dropped this," he said, holding out the familiar yellow scarf.

I glanced at Flo's naked neck. "Thank you," I said, taking the bandana and looking up into the man's face. It was Roger Wentworth in all his gorgeousness. He hardly paused as he continued toward the temple with a duffle bag strapped over his shoulder. I almost dropped my jaw, watching him enter through the front door and disappear into that place of happy people.

Roger Wentworth is a Mormon—a duffle-toting Mormon!
Stunned, I hardly minded Flo dragging me down the sidewalk.
"Did you see that, Flo? Roger Wentworth went inside the temple! Wow!"

I could have danced a happy jig. He was not only the mysterious Mr. Wentworth, but also the card-carrying-mysterious-Mormon Roger Wentworth. Hope swelled within me.

I stopped abruptly but Flo didn't, so I nearly ended up facedown on the sidewalk. Anyway, my thoughts went something like this: *Why should that give me hope? He's never noticed me. I know nothing about him except that he buys a lot of chocolate, wears a suit to work, and is a bona-fide Latter-day Saint.*

Flo finished dragging me around the temple and soon led me back into the courtyard of Taylor Palms. It's a fenced-in lawn in front of the three apartments on the property. I unhooked the leash and let Flo run free for a minute or two. I noticed that the FOR RENT sign that had been posted for two months was now gone from the window of the apartment across from mine.

The last family who lived there disappeared one night without even an adios. Much of the Hispanic population left town after the Arizona legislature passed the Fair and Legal Employment Act. Rent signs popped up all over our heavily Hispanic neighborhood. I considered moving too, to a more affluent area, for I'd saved up a sizeable down payment for a house, but I wasn't quite ready to leave the shadow of the temple. Seeing that glowing white edifice each night brought me peace and hope—and security.

I called Kylee and blurted my discovery about Roger.

"This is the perfect chance, Janie," she said. "He'll be inside for about two hours. Be there between 9:00 and 9:30 when he comes out."

I sank back into the couch. "What good will that do?"

"He'll be on a spiritual high. Maybe he'll see you and he'll know you are the one."

"Yeah, high hopes. Like that's going to happen." No man except John had ever given me as much as a second look.

"Well, then maybe he'll recognize you from the store and stop to talk."

"He has hardly even glanced at me *in* the store. No way will he recognize me," I said indignantly. "I'm not a stalker."

At 9:00 PM, I—Stalker Janie—sat dogless on the stone bench at the west entrance of the temple. Patrons exited through the front doors, one or two at a time, every few minutes. I waited. No Roger. At 9:20, an older woman with a bouncing girl about four years old came from the south parking lot. The sun had set hours before, but the girl ran on the plush lawn and stopped to *oooh* over each sleeping blossom in the flower bed. The woman sat on the stone bench at the foot of the temple entrance. I watched, amused.

The child called, "Come see a yellow flower."

The woman didn't move. "The flowers are sleeping, Emily. Let them sleep. You must be sleepy too. Yes?"

The girl ignored the question and ran to the reflection pool. "Can we go swimming?"

"May we," the woman corrected.

"May we go swimming?"

"We don't swim here. This is Heavenly Father's house." She patted the stone bench beside her. "Stop running around and come sit down."

Emily ignored the woman again and ran off to climb the stairs. She saw him before I did and made it to the top as Roger pushed his way through the revolving door. The little girl grabbed his hand. "Daddy! We came to take you home."

Daddy? This is his daughter? I hadn't considered the possibility that he had a child. Did that also mean he was married? I had, of course, noticed that he never wore a wedding ring.

Roger picked up Emily, carried her down the stairs, and briefly kissed the woman on the cheek. I was too far away to hear what he said to her. Then he set the girl on her feet and hand in hand, they walked with the woman to the parking lot. Emily chattered the whole distance. I stayed on the bench until they were out of sight.

Now I knew one more thing about Roger "Mystery" Wentworth. He had a child. He was, or had been married, and there was an older woman, maybe a mother or an aunt, in his life.

With a sigh, I left the bench, then walked across the street to my cottage, dragging my feet. I stood in the empty courtyard, wondering who had rented the unit facing mine. Perhaps another Hispanic family who didn't speak English.

I had lingered outside too long, for Florentine whimpered on the other side of the door.

"Flo, it's me." I opened the door to my dog and her joyfully wagging tail. Next thing I knew, she had her paws on my shoulders and was kissing me. Say goodbye to all the makeup specially applied an hour ago. It did me no good anyway.

I dried my face with one of the many slobber rags I kept handy around the cottage. Though the place was tiny, and the one being in all the world who loved me most is covered in short hair and is four-footed, this was home.

FIVE

Hush, Jane! you think too much of the love of human beings; you are too impulsive, too vehement; the sovereign hand that created your frame, and put life into it, has provided you with other resources than your feeble self.

It was another week before I saw Roger Wentworth again. He came in at 9:00 sharp on Tuesday morning while I was alone in the shop. "Good morning," I greeted, trying to be cheerful. How many times had I attempted to sound upbeat in the past year so that he'd take a moment and actually look at me? And had he? Guess again.

"I'd like your Signature rose wrapped and delivered to Eden's Garden."

"As usual," I said. A new line. I'd never used that before.

I could tell the line surprised him because he looked up. Our eyes met briefly. He looked away. "Uh, yes." He went to look over the display cases. "And—" he said as I waited "—something different. What do you have that's new?"

I tapped on the top of the glass case. "This Alice in Wonderland. I just finished the design last week."

He studied the three-inch Alice. She stood with feet together, arms extended, with one hand holding her skirt. "I'll take it. Will you put it in a box?"

I nodded. I *always* put his items in a box. I wanted so much to say more to him—something meaningful—but what? "Oh, by the way, I saw you at the temple last week"? Did I dare ask prying questions such as, "Are you married?" and "Who is Winnie Wentworth?" How about, "Will you spend some time with me? How about eternity?"

I reprimanded myself by glancing at the company logo on my apron. None of those questions sounded professional, and our goal is to treat our customers professionally at all times. This infatuation thing was getting out of hand.

I wrapped the rose in pink tissue and placed it carefully in a box. Then I took a smaller box from the shelf for Alice. If I ever hoped for even a friendly relationship with Roger Wentworth, I'd have to take a tiny step over that professional line—logo or no logo. *Courage, girl.* I took a deep breath.

"Is this for your daughter?" I asked, looking up.

His dark eyebrows knit before he responded. "I—well, yes." He coughed.

So, I'd made him uncomfortable by acting too familiar. I wanted to watch him squirm some more.

I put a small piece of tissue in the box, and then gently set Alice on the tissue. "How old is she?"

Roger nearly choked on the answer. "She's . . . four."

I placed the lid on the box and put the box into a white insulated bag. He handed me his debit card and waited while I made the transaction. I pulled the pen from the pocket of my apron and handed it to him to sign the slip.

"Four is a fun age," I said. It sounded friendly, I thought.

"Yes." He took the bag and left. I watched him, wondering

if the day would ever come that he would loosen up and stay a moment longer to talk.

I haven't said much about Tessa and Frank Ship. They take over on Friday and Saturday evenings, the only evenings the shop stays open. They enjoy the dinner hour's clientele and are saving up to take a Mediterranean cruise. Frank is a tall, white-haired seventy-year-old whose specialty is unique cake decorating. So, by Friday at 5:00—after a week of getting up early—I have the cakes ready and turn the shop over to the Ships. Then I go home happily, knowing I can sleep until noon the next day if I want.

Anyway, Saturday dawned. I stayed snuggled in bed with the curtains open and watched high, wispy clouds drift across the blue Arizona sky, and went over the schedule for the day. My life was all mine until 1:00 when I had to be in the shop. Carmen and Cricket opened at 10:00 AM. Willa and I would take over at 2:00 PM until Tessa and Frank came at 5:00 PM. All set.

The roar of a truck motor outside my window startled me into reality. I looked out and saw *U-HAUL* in large letters

"The new renters are here," I told Flo, who had also been awakened and was already bouncing between the door and the window. "There's no one else to do it, so we might as well be the welcoming committee."

I got up and pulled on a wrinkled jogging suit. It didn't qualify as a suit because the top and pants didn't match, but so what? "Como esta," I practiced my Spanish. "Mi nombre es Rosa." Then, deciding to be merciful to anyone who might see me, I dragged a brush through my dark brown hair and coerced it into a semi-decent ponytail. Then I looked closer in the mirror and rubbed away smudged mascara from beneath my gorgeous blue eyes. Good enough. No need for makeup. A banana and a glass of milk did just fine as breakfast.

I opened the door in time to dodge an armoire. Seriously, it almost ran me down! The man in front bore a remarkable resemblance to Roger Wentworth, only he was shorter. I had Roger on the brain, though, so I decided the resemblance was only a coincidence. The man shouldering the other end of the armoire was taller and looked even more like Roger. My stomach suddenly hurt. Maybe I shouldn't have wolfed down that banana so fast. Tingles ran through me and the weather wasn't even cold. (Remember, this is Arizona in September.) I knew the second man couldn't be Roger, but still, he had the same build, stood the same height, and had the same hair color and style. If it wasn't Roger, then it was his twin.

The men carried the armoire right through the open front door of the vacant apartment. That's when I saw that profile I'd grown so crazy about.

My knees went feeble and I stepped back into my cottage, tripping on the rug just inside the door. I went into the bathroom, ripped the band out of my hair, combed out the last tangles, and redid the ponytail. Then I washed off the rest of yesterday's makeup and applied some powder foundation and blush. That didn't look much better.

I went back to the door—which I had left open—and now Flo was across the courtyard, barking and wagging her tail like an overgrown puppy. She was ecstatic when the men came out of the apartment and headed toward the moving van. Of course, she followed.

I remained out of sight until they passed my door, and then ordered, "Flo! Here, girl!" She bounced a few times more and then stopped to consider me, obviously deciding if she would obey my command. "Flo!" I called louder. "Come, girl!"

It was just too hard for a canine—deciding between

potentially new friends or obeying her mistress. Flo looked back and forth once, twice, and on the third, she bounded past the moving van and into the street.

"For heaven's sake!" I mumbled and grabbed a leash from the rack behind the door. Roger and friend had climbed into the back of the van and were wrestling with a queen-size mattress. No way did I want him seeing me with very little makeup and wearing sloppy old sweats.

"Flo! Come home, now!" She ignored the command and circumvented me, bounding up into the van. Then my dog jumped up and put her paws on the chest of the man of my dreams—and licked his face as if he were a giant lollipop.

Ignoring the ramp, I climbed into the van and started apologizing profusely. Flo thumped me several times with her hyper tail before I could get the leash attached to the collar. "I'm sorry. I'm so sorry," I kept repeating while trying to drag the dog out of the van. But she wouldn't budge.

With his bare hand, Roger tried to wipe the thick slobber from his face. Flo bounced once more, knocking down the mattress. I took hold of the leash. Glass shattered.

Not stopping to look, I dragged the reluctant dog down the ramp and several yards to my still-open front door. I managed to get her inside and push the door closed behind me. With my back against the door, and in frustration, I slid to the floor. How was Roger Wentworth ever going to think of me seriously after a fiasco like that? I was doomed!

My furry friend wasn't giving up so easily. She went to the window and barked. I'm sure it was a plea for her new friends to come rescue her.

"Flo, settle down!"

Then came a knock. Followed by her ecstatically wagging tail, the Great Dane ran over me to get to the door. "They're not here to liberate you," I assured her. "They probably want to haul you off to the pound, after what you did."

I reached up and opened the door only a crack, using my leg to bar the dog from going outside. (Remember, I still sat on the floor.) Flo did manage to get her head out. There stood Roger's look-alike towering above me. "Excuse me, ma'am."

Ma'am? Do I look that old?

"My brother is moving in across the way." As he motioned to the vacant apartment, his gold wedding ring flashed. "Could I borrow a broom to clean up the glass from the accident your, uh, dog just caused?" I knew he only blamed the dog to be polite, since it was my fault she didn't obey me.

"Oh, sure. I'm so sorry about that! I'll have to shut the door while I find it." I shoved the door closed and got to my feet. While Flo barked at the doorknob, I went to the kitchen closet and pulled out the broom and dustpan. "Settle down, girl!" I ordered.

When I opened the door, Flo stuck her nose out again. (That is her version of getting a foot in or out the door.) Controlling this dog is, I'm sure, equivalent to Olympic training, and even though I have developed muscles, I struggled to hold her back while handing the man the broom. "I'm so sorry about the dog, and the mess and all."

"Could we also get some ice water? Your dog knocked over and broke my brother's drinking glasses, and the water hasn't been turned on in the apartment anyway, and we still have quite a bit to unload."

"Sure." I looked down at the elated dog. "It's the least I can do after . . . How about I bring it out to you?"

He agreed.

I pulled the dog out of the way and closed the door, and then glared at Flo with all the grimness I could muster. So much for a dog being a girl's best friend!

Nearly stepping on my feet, Flo followed me to the kitchen. I filled two glasses with ice and cold water, and carried them to the door. Flo thought she was going outside again because I could see it in her big, gray eyes. "Flo, you've got to stay inside while I take this out to Roger." She stepped up to the door, obviously anticipating it opening. "You're not going," I insisted.

Placing the glasses on the dining table, I led the canine to the bedroom. She happily bounced onto the bed, thinking it was another game. Never suspecting the game was called Close the Door and Lock the Dog in the Room, she bounded off the bed and hit the door with her big paws. Then there was only heavy breathing, and, I assume, a dog with a confused look on her face.

"You'll be fine. Just wait here."

I grabbed the glasses of water and started toward the moving van. I stood straight, pulled in my tummy, and lifted my chin. This was my chance and I had to make it good. Roger Wentworth would certainly notice a girl bringing ice-cold, refreshing water on a hot day. I rounded the corner with a big smile.

Roger had his back turned, talking on a cell phone in a heated conversation.

"Oh, thank you!" the look-alike said, coming toward me and taking both glasses. "My brother is on the phone. I'll give this to him when he's done. Should we set the empty glasses outside your door?"

"No! I want Roger to personally return them and gush about how thankful he is!" was what I wanted to say, but "Uh—all right" was my brilliant reply. My smile faded into oblivion. I walked back to my cottage, closed the door, dropped my chin, and let my tummy hang. Dang! As far as RW was concerned, I was still invisible.

Roger and his brother passed my door at least a zillion times that morning. No longer a prisoner in the bedroom, Flo put her nose to the window and whimpered. (Now you know why I buy a lot of Windex.) I peeked through the curtains occasionally, like a spy, and I admit I whimpered like Flo, but just a little. This was the first time I had seen Roger Wentworth wearing casual clothes, and he still rated way over the charts on handsome.

They brought in two dressers, a canopy bed, and, finally, a four-foot-tall pink dollhouse.

The presence of the dollhouse proved that his daughter *was* coming. And the older woman, too? I doubted it, using my limited logic. It was only a two-bedroom apartment. Maybe the older woman was a grandmother or a nanny. It appeared it would only be Roger and his daughter. This would prove to be interesting—I was sure of it.

After hearing the van drive away, I found the glasses on the doorstep. *Which glass did he drink from?* I wondered, hesitating before setting them in the dishwasher. *You foolish girl! What a waste to get your hopes up on a man who will never look at you. Maybe he is married. Nah,* I reasoned. *Any woman would want to have a say in the arrangement of the furniture in a new apartment. Maybe he's divorced and has sworn off women. Maybe—*

The whole Roger thing was driving me crazy. I needed to get my mind off him, so I did what I always do. I called Kylee.

"He's moved in next door, and he brought a pink dollhouse."

"Who?" Kylee asked.

"Roger Wentworth!" Why wasn't she on the same track with me?

"Janie, are you all right? Do you mean *our* Roger Wentworth?"

"I mean *the* one and only, now-my-neighbor Roger Wentworth."

"I don't believe it. He's moved in next door? Well, girl, get started baking cookies like a good neighbor!"

SIX

Suppose he should be absent spring, summer, and autumn: how joyless sunshine and fine days will seem!

Sunday, I didn't see Roger. I left my curtains open to try to catch a glimpse of him walking by. The cookies I'd made were getting older by the minute.

Our tiny apartment complex has three units. Mrs. Carter lives in number 1, the middle apartment that sits the farthest back but faces the street. She travels between Mesa and the Family History Library in Salt Lake City. I think she eats, drinks, and dreams genealogy. I've even overheard her tell of dead ancestors visiting her in the night. Now that's spooky! I haven't seen Mrs. Carter or her Taurus for a while, so I assume she is in Utah.

My apartment (I mean, my cottage) faces the same direction but sits closer to the street. Roger's sits perpendicular to the street, and we all share the courtyard.

Monday evening, the lights burned in apartment number 2. When Flo and I were returning from our evening walk, a little girl's giggle escaped through an open window. A brand new blue Prius was parked in number 2's reserved parking spot. It felt like a warm fuzzy to hear that high-pitched laughter and to know I had neighbors and wasn't alone. Thinking of taking the cookies to Roger, I pulled one out from beneath the plastic wrap. *Stale.* Now I had no excuse to go visiting.

By morning when I left for the chocolate shop, the Prius was gone and apartment number 2 was quiet.

I walked into the shop to the smell of roasting cacao beans. What a welcome aroma! I opened the shop at 7:30 as the cracking machine and the grinder buzzed. (We open early to serve people on their way to work.) Alice in Wonderland sold out during the morning rush, so I prepared the mold for pouring. I also set out the Arizona State mold and the saguaro cactus mold, since the tourist season starts in October and out-of-state visitors love these two designs.

I own almost sixty molds, twenty of which I designed myself. One of my favorites is a businessman in a Superman stance, fists on waist, suit coat open, and tie flying. I call it Superdad. By no accident, it resembles Roger—remarkably well, I must say. I finished the mold in time to display Superdad at the Tempe Arts Festival. He makes a perfect Father's Day gift. The year before, I won first place in the chocolate contest for a laughing mushroom, but that's another story.

My mother had artistic talents. As a little girl, I loved to sit and watch her sculpt in clay. She dabbled at it only as a hobby, and she gave away most of her work. My father worked his way through college in a candy factory. He'd get us laughing by telling us about his taffy-pulling misadventures. Put an artist and a confectioner together, and the result is me. (I don't know where the accountant in Kylee came from.)

Now, where am I in my story? Oh, yeah. I came into the shop and breathed in the delectable aroma of roasting cacao beans. The next half hour passed quietly, and we only made a few sales. I poured chocolate into the molds, getting so busy that I forgot the time. When my stomach started flipping out with butterflies, I looked up at the clock. Exactly 8:58. I listened. No tingling door chime.

Nine o'clock came and went with no Roger Wentworth. Kylee arrived and started on the books. I waited longer, holding on to hope that the handsome face I had grown accustomed to would show, but every time the door chime rang, I'd look up only to discover it wasn't him. With each non-Roger customer, the butterflies fluttered less and I realized he probably would not grace my threshold that day.

By noon I was in the depths of disappointment. This was the first time in . . . I tried to think of how many months that gorgeous man with the sad eyes had been walking into my shop every Tuesday at 9:00 AM and ordering a solo chocolate flower.

Before Kylee left to pick up her children from school, she told me, "I've got a doctor's appointment later—another specialist."

"But Kylee, if you have another baby, you'll spend less time in the shop. What will I do?"

"Hmm. Why worry about something that may never happen?"

I felt bad for thinking only of myself.

"I have an idea," Kylee said. "You get married and have a baby, and then we can trade off babysitting and running the store."

"Uh-huh. And who will I marry?" Roger Wentworth immediately came to mind. *Yeah, like that will ever happen.*

"You're a pretty girl, Janie Rose, and you have a lot to offer a man—great personality, strong faith in the gospel, a good heart, artistic talent, and so many other wonderful qualities. Have faith and don't give up hope, okay?"

So I promised myself to never give up hope. *Maybe when I'm as old as Aunt Lucy,* I thought, *those little old men on the front row of the chapel will look better to me.*

After Kylee left, business still didn't pick up. At 3:00, the phone rang. I answered. "Chocolate Art Forever. This is Janie speaking."

"Yes. This is Roger Wentworth." My stomach lurched at the sound of his masculine voice. I reached for a pen.

"I'd like to order one Signature rose to be delivered."

"To Eden's Garden?"

"No." There was a pause. "I won't be sending them to the hospital anymore." He gave me a new address in north Mesa, along with a debit card number.

"I'll send it out today," I said. "And will the name be Winnie Wentworth?"

"Yes, Winnie Wentworth." He sounded surprised that I had assumed. Oh, no! Did he suspect that our shop revolved around his Tuesday visits?

He thanked me and hung up without a goodbye.

Willa, our afternoon help, walked in. She is twenty years old, six feet tall, and weighs, on heavier days, one hundred and twenty pounds. She grew up in a family of bronco riders. I've never confessed to her that I hired her to be a bouncer, just in case. That walking zipper (when she turns sideways, she almost disappears) has a black belt in karate and no fear. She even mastered fire eating. The month before, spelunking rocked her world. Her master-the-difficult mentality has led her to indulge in rappelling, scuba diving, parachuting, skateboarding, tightrope walking . . . You name it and she has tried it. Her motto is probably The greater the risk, the better.

I turned the front of the store over to Willa and took the rose to the kitchen to prepare it for delivery. Even though Willa is young, I don't really have to worry. Anyone who tries to take advantage of her youth soon finds out she can hold her own. For instance, one day a middle-aged man tried to get out of the shop without paying. Willa finished packaging his order and the phone rang. As she answered it, he grabbed the bag and headed toward the door, but Willa jumped over the counter and tackled him before he could reach it.

I finished tying the last bow on the package and I heard Willa say, "Sorry, I can't give out that information." Actually, her tone sounded more like a growl. "I don't know who you are or what you want, but we respect the privacy of our customers!"

Clearly, Willa had forgotten our rule to treat customers professionally at all times! I set down the box and hurried into the shop. "Is there a problem?"

She turned her back to the counter, rolled her eyes toward the customer, and spoke through clamped teeth. "She claims to be Wentworth's sister."

Willa had only seen Roger Wentworth a few times when she happened to be in the shop during school breaks. He is a household name with us (or should I say shop-hold name?), and she appreciated his ability to stay mysterious.

I glanced at the woman. She had dark rings under her eyes and wore a plunging ruffled neckline over a too-short black skirt and bare legs. Her stringy blonde hair begged for a rendezvous with Pert Plus, and the odor of cigarettes masked the Chanel No. 5 she wore, though she undoubtedly hoped for the opposite effect.

"May I help you?" I asked.

"Yeah." She stepped up confidently and dropped a crinkled photo onto the counter. "I'm looking for this guy." She grasped the strap of her shoulder bag tighter. "I know he comes in here. He's kinda skipped out on me and, like, he kinda owes me."

"Kinda?" I looked at the snapshot. Even though it wasn't a Superman stance or any kind of a posed shot, I recognized Roger. I didn't know what this woman wanted, but she surely didn't talk about him like a sister would. "I haven't seen him today."

From her expression, I could tell she thought I was lying. "Have ya ever seen him? He comes here, right?"

She reminded me of a starved alley cat, and my gut feeling was to not feed her. I picked up the photo and handed it to her. "He's been in here a few times, but not for a week, at least." It wasn't a lie.

"I'm kinda desperate to get a hold of him. Ya see, I'm his—" her eyes shifted to Willa "—his sister." The woman held no resemblance to Roger or his look-alike brother, so her claim was clearly a lie unless she was adopted. "Do ya know his number, or where he lives—or anything that could help me?"

Anything that could help you? Yeah, a bar of soap.

"Please? Can you help me find my brother?"

You think I'm that gullible? I prayed that God would forgive my dishonesty. "I'm sorry, but I can't. Our customers don't give us that kind of information, but" —I pulled paper and a pen from the drawer beneath the counter and pushed them toward her— "I'll give him your number if he comes again."

"No." The woman stepped back. "I'll find him on my own. It's an emergency." She turned abruptly and wiggled out of the store, her miniskirt barely covering her derrière. She let the door slam behind her and the chime screamed.

"How do you like that?" Willa said, watching her. "She's really gutsy."

"You don't think she's his sister?"

"No way! Roger Wentworth is saintly. That women seems like pure evil."

I walked back to the kitchen and Willa followed. "So, Mr. Wentworth didn't show up today?" she asked. "Do you think something's wrong?"

"He called and ordered the flower to be delivered. It wasn't to the hospital, though. It's an address in Mesa."

Willa looked thoughtful. She plopped her 120 pounds on the rickety stool. "Maybe he got busy or he's sick."

I knew Willa was just as infatuated with Wentworth as I was. I lowered my voice. "Roger has a daughter and they moved in next door to me this weekend."

Willa's jaw dropped. "What? Why didn't you tell me that yesterday?"

"Monday's your day off."

"Well, then you could have called."

Called? "Do you even answer your cell phone while skydiving?"

Linc walked in and tossed the van keys on the hook. "It just doesn't seem like Tuesday without making a run to the hospital. Has Wentworth come in yet?"

"No," Willa sulked, still sitting on the stool. "We miss him."

"But he called," I said. "Hey, Linc. I know you get off work right now, but can you make a run to north Mesa to deliver this rose to Winnie Wentworth?" I explained that Roger had given me a new address.

Linc looked at his watch. "Sure can't. My mama is expecting me to take her over to Aunt Gertie's by five. You know how those dual airbags love their weekly visit. I gotta get goin'." He traded the logo hat for his beanie from the rack and headed out the door.

"Willa?" I asked.

She looked apologetic. "I'm sorry, but I have a date to go bungee jumping as soon as I leave here. He's hot, too—tall and tan." She sighed. "Besides, I don't drive the truck if I don't have to."

I looked at her in wonder. "You'll go bungee jumping, but you won't drive the truck?"

With all its nicks and dents and half-missing fender, our delivery truck looks like a wounded veteran of WWII. Besides its looks, you have to know how to hold the key just right to get it started. At least I don't worry about leaving it in the back alley overnight. No one could steal it. No one would *want* to steal it. And it is sort of a death trap.

"All right," I said. "I'll make Mr. Wentworth's delivery. If he wasn't such a faithful customer, I'd leave it for Linc to deliver in the morning." I gathered my things together. "Can you hold down the fort for an hour?" Willa nodded. I knew I could trust her. "Kylee will be back soon to close up."

I bypassed the truck and headed for my SUV. (I have to own a big car to carry my dog in.) I agree with Willa—if I don't have to drive the old, battered jalopy, I won't.

The traffic on Loop 202 wasn't too busy yet, so getting to the east valley took only fifteen minutes. The exit was wide open at Val Vista, and I followed the road southward. When I found the address, I turned into the tree-lined driveway but was stopped after a few feet by a tall gate. An equally high wrought-iron fence surrounded the property. Looking past the fence, I saw my destination. On the other side of the gate, hidden from the street by vines and cypress trees, stood an enormous tiled-roof house with a two-story-high entry.

I leaned forward. "Wow!" I said in awe, getting a full view

of the mansion. I pulled up to a control island, lowered the car window, and hit the intercom button.

In a moment a woman's voice answered. "May I help you?"

"I have a delivery for Winnie Wentworth from Chocolate Art Forever." I heard a click, and the gate immediately rolled aside. *Impressive.* I drove through the gate, which closed behind me, and I parked in front of the house.

Out of the car and with box in hand, I looked again at the huge house. "I'd hate to be the one who cleans this place," I muttered to myself.

When I heard fumbling with locks, I hurried to the door. A petite Asian woman in pink scrubs that bore the embroidered name "Grace" over the left pocket, pulled open the door wide enough that I could see into the house. *Martha Stewart must live here,* I thought to myself. The place was immaculate, the carpets a vibrant white, and the interior had a talented decorator's touch.

"Please, come in. Mr. Wentworth told me you'd be coming."

I tried to see over the woman's head as I stepped over the threshold, but I saw no one else. Grace closed the door.

"Please, sign here for it." I pointed to a line on the clipboard. "How is Winnie today?" *Why did I say that? I could kick myself. I don't even know the woman!*

Grace didn't flinch. "She's doing better." She handed back the clipboard and I left.

Back in my car, I followed the circular drive around to the gate. It opened by an electric eye and I drove onto the street. *What is this all about—the mansion, Winnie, and the weekly delivery?* I could only speculate, but in reality, Winnie's life, Roger's life, and their relationship was none of my business. I needed to remain professional and stick to my own business—

the business of providing beautiful chocolate creations to those who can appreciate and pay for them.

But as hard as I tried, my mind kept returning to Roger Wentworth and his mysterious Winnie. Was she his mother? His wife? Was she a sister, or something else that my prying little mind hadn't thought of yet?

When I arrived home, the door to Roger's apartment stood slightly ajar, and voices from a television drifted on the late afternoon air. I unlocked my front door and Flo met me literally face to face, almost knocking me over. She pushed past me, bounced across the courtyard, and ran right through Roger's open door.

"No!" I cried, but I couldn't get to his door fast enough. Then I heard a child's scream. "Oh, no," I groaned, imagining the worst.

When I reached the door and looked in, Flo sat calmly on her hind legs while a small girl stood next to her with her arms wrapped around the dog's neck. Roger reached the room as I reached the door, and we both stared at the sight.

The child turned to Roger. "He's my friend."

"It looks that way." Roger glanced at me, then back to his daughter. "Emily, let the lady take her dog home."

I laughed. "I'm in no hurry," I said to Roger. "It looks like you've made a friend—again."

Emily tightened her hold on Flo, and the dog sighed her enjoyment. Emily giggled and then kissed Flo below the ear. "What's his name?"

"*Her* name is Florentine, but I just call her Flo."

"It's a girl?" Emily giggled, stepped back, and got a better look at the dog. "What is she wearing on her neck?"

"It's a bandana," Roger said. Then he looked at me. "She's a beautiful dog." He knelt down by his daughter and stroked

Flo's neck. "Come on, Emily. Let the nice lady take her dog home. You can visit again tomorrow. She lives right next door."

I don't know why I was surprised that he knew where I lived, especially after the moving fiasco. Nevertheless, I took the hint. "Come, Flo," I said in my most authoritative voice.

Flo didn't budge.

"I want her to stay," Emily pouted.

Flo stayed.

Roger stood and walked over to me. "Nice dog."

"Not really. She broke every glass you own. Remember?"

"No problem. I've replaced them." He put out his hand. "I'm Roger and this is my daughter Emily."

I shook his hand. "And I'm Janie. I'm glad to meet you."

After that I took Flo home.

Finally, we officially met.

Finally.

SEVEN

The ease of his manner freed me from painful restraint; the friendly frankness, as correct as cordial, with which he treated me, drew me to him.

Roger kept his word and allowed Emily to come outdoors the next evening. Flo and I didn't go for our walk, but stayed in the courtyard and played with the little girl. To my disappointment, Roger remained inside his apartment. I taught Emily to throw the slobbery rawhide bone so Flo could retrieve it. There is no better therapy than to watch a child romp with a dog. What do children and dogs have in common? I have pondered that question and my conclusion is that they both love unconditionally.

I've lived with roommates in my time, but let me assure you, there's no better roommate than a dog. They don't borrow money or wear your clothes. They don't eat your favorite chocolate when you aren't home—unless you leave it out, of course, which could be fatal to the dog. You don't have to remind them to pay their share of the rent. Best of all, they don't compete for the man you love.

Flo and Emily were crazy about each other, so why weren't the other two of this foursome hitting it off as well? I wished Roger would come out and talk. He left the front door open and looked out occasionally to check on Emily, whereupon I'd smile and give an everything-is-fine wave. But he never came out to chat.

So much for thinking that living so close would present me with golden opportunities. Even though I was outdoors with the whole world buzzing around me, I felt alone because the only man I wanted to notice me, didn't.

I didn't see Roger again until the next Tuesday, when he came into the shop right on schedule. When he walked in, I could tell he hadn't expected to see me, of all people, behind the counter.

It happened like this: Roger glanced up at the posted prices and began telling me his order. "I'd like one chocolate rose to be sent to this address." He handed me a card and that's when he actually looked at me. I smiled. He focused and a look of recognition claimed his eyes, chasing the sadness from them only briefly.

"Hello—" His brow furrowed. "Is it Janie?"

"Yes. Hello, Roger."

He looked embarrassed. "I—well." He rubbed his forehead and smiled. "You look different without your Great Dane."

"Thinner?"

Ignoring my sarcastic comment, he looked around. "Have you always worked here?"

"I own this shop. I'm usually here Tuesday mornings." *Always. I wouldn't miss it.* I pulled a box from the stack and lined it with pink tissue paper. "How is Emily today?"

He smiled again. "She's fine. The first thing she wanted to do this morning was see Flo."

"Emily is welcome anytime. I know Flo is the size of Mount Everest, but she is actually a very gentle dog."

"As I've seen. A very friendly dog, too, especially on moving day."

"Yeah, well—" I knew I still owed him big time for that one.

Roger nervously cracked his knuckles. "You are good to spend time with my daughter."

"It's fun for me, since I don't have children of my own." I took a chocolate rose from the display case and placed it carefully in the box. "Flo and I are usually home in the evenings, except when I go visiting teaching." Did he catch the huge Mormon hint there? I tucked the tissue around the rose. "We'd be happy to watch Emily anytime you need to go out. She could join us for our walk around the temple. *You* could join us too, for that matter." I signed the box.

"Thank you. I'll keep that in mind." He stepped over to the novelty case. "Now something for Emily. What's new?"

"Have you taken her the Great Dane?" I pointed to the dog figure.

He smiled. My heart fluttered.

"Emily will love it," he said.

"It's Flo. I used her as the model. Well, actually she wouldn't hold still. Have you ever tried to use a dog for a model?"

Roger looked at bit confused, so I decided I'd better quit rambling. I took the tiny dog from the case, wrapped it in tissue, and placed it in a small box. After charging Roger's debit card, I returned the card and handed him the box. "So, tonight about 8:00?" *Look at me, Miss Forward, making a date!*

"I, uh—" He looked flustered. "Maybe Emily can go with you, but she usually goes to bed at 8:00."

You're not getting off that easily. "I close up at 6:30 and will be home about 7:00. Let's go then. Flo will love going an hour earlier." I'd close at 4:00 if it meant getting to spend time with Roger.

He still looked doubtful. "Well, not tonight."

My cheeks burned as my heart dropped to my toes and rolled onto the floor. He stepped on it as he walked out the door.

The chime rang, reminding me of the sound of Cinderella's fairy godmother's magic wand. It wasn't that I related to Cinderella—it's just that it would take more than magic to put my broken heart back together.

"Tonight" came and Flo and I took our walk alone. We'd usually go by ourselves, so why did I feel so lonely? It would be invigorating to have a four-year-old bouncing along with us, excited about sleeping flowers and an oversized dog. And it would be so pleasant having a grown man walking beside me, protecting me—well, that's what I have a big dog for—and to have human conversation with.

When Flo and I got back to the cottage, the lights glowed at Roger's place. We stopped on our porch just as Emily's bedroom light flicked off. I assumed she was snuggling down for the night and going to sleep. Flo looked at me with sad eyes.

The truth is, we felt left out. I turned the key and let us in, sat on the couch, turned on the TV, and flipped through the channels. Nothing. I turned it off. Flo stretched out on her rug and sighed.

"What's wrong with us, Flo? We've been happy living alone for years, and now that the Wentworths have moved in, we have nothing to do."

Flo sighed again.

I picked up the *Ensign* and tried to get interested in an article about being single and happy, which I kept handy for such moments, but this time it brought no solace.

I picked up *National Geographic Adventure* and read an article that encouraged people to try bungee jumping, but I knew I wouldn't. I closed the magazine, went to the kitchen, and grabbed a stale cookie, but I knew I shouldn't. So I tossed the whole batch into the wastebasket and sighed.

"I guess we might as well get ready for bed," I told Flo and headed toward the bedroom.

Bang, bang, bang! The noise came from across the courtyard. I heard men's voices and went to the window and parted the curtains. There on Roger's doorstep were two uniformed police officers.

EIGHT

"My little friend!" said he, "I wish I were in a quiet island with only you; and trouble, and danger, and hideous recollections removed from me."

"Can I help you, sir?—I'd give my life to serve you."

"Jane, if aid is wanted, I'll seek it at your hands; I promise you that."

"Thank you, sir. Tell me what to do,—I'll try . . . to do it."

Feeling like a spy, I opened the door a crack, held my breath, and listened, but I couldn't make out any words the two policemen were saying. They spoke in low tones, and I could tell they were giving Roger unexpected information, because he kept nodding his head as he listened. After a minute, the officers left. Roger leaned against the doorframe and rubbed his forehead while he looked into the star-scarce sky for several moments.

Before Roger came to live across my courtyard, I would have said that "attractive" and "faded jeans" did not belong in the same category, but at this moment, I realized I was wrong. He looked so handsome standing in the dim porch light in his almost-threadbare jeans. He looked anguished and so helpless at that moment. I wished I could take him in my arms and hold him until all his hurt went away.

I opened my door. "Is everything all right?" I dared call to him. He looked around to see who had spoken, and when he saw me standing in the light of the open door, he walked across the lawn toward me.

"Could you stay with Emily for an hour or so? I have some urgent business I must take care of." He met my eyes and for a moment, I thought he would have welcomed my arms. I stepped closer.

"Sure. Is everything all right?" I placed a hand on his arm.

"Everything is fine." He broke from my gaze, from my touch, and fumbled in his pocket. "I think Emily is still awake." He pulled out a ring of keys and took one off. "Here is an extra key to my place—for emergencies."

For a moment, I just stared at the unexpected offering. Roger went back into his apartment and I finally came out of my shock, went to get my own key, and locked my cottage. Flo and I walked across the lawn and waited on Roger's porch.

In a moment, he came out again. "I shouldn't be too long."

"Hey," I said. "Don't worry about hurrying back. I'll just sleep on the couch if I need to. Take as long as you need."

Relief spread across his face, followed by a smile that made my heart do a little flip.

"Thanks," Roger said. "I put a pillow on the couch for you. You're great to help me. It might be later, then."

Awkwardly, he put out his hand for a handshake. I took it and enjoyed the contact even though it was much too brief. Then he sprinted toward his car.

I felt uncomfortable walking into Roger's place. Flo waited in the doorway, obviously wondering why we were there, since she couldn't see Emily. I looked around. A pillow lay on the couch, and a short hall passed two doors and led to a bathroom.

Soon, a tiny figure appeared in the hallway. "Janie? Where's my Daddy?"

"He had to leave." I knelt on the linoleum next to her and signaled Flo to come. "Do you want to dog-sit?"

When she saw Flo, Emily squealed and threw her arms around the dog's neck. "Flo!" She looked up at me. "But Flo is too big for me to sit on."

I giggled at her naivety. "Then let's sit on the couch."

I took Emily's hand, pushed the pillow aside, and sat. Emily crawled up beside me and smoothed her other hand over the dog's head. If Flo had been a cat, she would have purred.

The room was sparsely furnished: the couch, a TV on a small stand, a bookshelf, and one overstuffed chair. On the shelf sat some books and a framed photograph. Walking over, I picked up the frame and studied the picture. It was Roger and a stunning brunette, both smiling. Happiness radiated from their eyes—a happiness I'd never seen in Roger before. I glanced at Emily, who was preoccupied with Flo. Traces of this woman's beauty shone in the little girl's face.

Emily's blond curls tumbled freely over the dog. "I love you, Flo," she said, putting her arms around the dog's neck. Flo glanced at me, panting contentedly and enjoying every moment of the attention.

I looked again at the woman in the photo. Was this Winnie? From her old-fashioned name, I had imagined Winnie as an older woman. No matter what had happened between Roger and this striking woman, I knew it caused the sadness that now dominated his eyes. I set the picture back on the shelf and noticed the children's books there. Grabbing the first few, I went back to sit with Emily. "Shall we read a book?"

Emily's curls bounced as she nodded. She let go of Flo and scooted back onto the couch, her feet barely reaching the edge.

She snuggled closer to me and took a book from the stack. Its cover showed a small dog in a pet-store window.

Emily opened it and pointed at the first picture. "This is about a little dog, not a big dog like Flo. The dog is in a pet store and wishes someone would come to buy him." She went on telling the story. My only job was to turn the pages. I read the next story, but long before the last page, Emily had slipped off to sleep.

I carried her into her bedroom where, lit by a dim nightlight, a frilly canopy bed filled half of the room. I laid her on the bed, trying not to wake her, and pulled the covers around her. She appeared to be peacefully sleeping, so I tiptoed out.

Yes, I am not only Stalker Janie, but Nosey Janie. My only excuse is that the other bedroom door stood wide open. Besides, I was curious about how Roger Wentworth lived. I wasn't surprised at the tidy room. A queen bed was made up in a simple brown bedspread and no frills, and there was a dresser, an open closet where several dress shirts hung, and a pair of men's dress shoes on the floor of the closet.

I leaned against the doorframe. Now I know this sounds sappy, but it did something to my heart to know that this very room was where the man with the sad eyes—the one who had made my heart thump every Tuesday at 9:00 AM for the last several months—slept. I wanted to dust, or fluff pillows—do *something* to make his life a little more comfortable, but I didn't dare go any further than the doorway.

Back on the couch, I flipped through the rest of the books while Flo serenaded me with her snoring. Finally, after dozing off several times, I picked up the pillow, put it at the end of the couch, and lay down with my head on the pillow, wondering if it had ever held *his* sleeping head. Silly, huh? I punched the pillow a few times and eventually got comfortable. A few more minutes and I slipped off to sleep.

The click of the doorknob startled me. Flo stood and stretched, and I sat up as Roger walked in.

He hesitated for a moment. "Sorry to wake you."

"You look as tired as I feel," I said groggily. I glanced at the clock on the wall—2:00 AM. Roger took a few steps into the cottage but left the door open. I knew it was my signal to leave.

"I'm so sorry to have kept you up all night like this. I'm sure you're busy."

"Yeah." I searched for a comeback. "I could have been sorting socks."

He laughed and almost seemed to relax a little. "You don't know how much I appreciate your staying with Emily. I don't know what I would have done if you hadn't—I guess I'd have taken her with me."

"Dragging a four-year-old around in the middle of the night can be an invigorating experience." That made him chuckle too. "I hope everything is fine." It was a question.

He looked away. "For now."

"As I offered in the shop today, I'll always help out when I can." I wished he would explain more. "I hope everything is all right." There I go again, repeating myself and sticking my nose where it doesn't belong.

Roger nodded. "Yes. Thank you for your help."

Flo and I left, and I noticed Roger didn't close his door until I had safely opened mine.

The air had taken on an unusual chill for early October.

In bed, I lay awake, unable to get my mind off Roger. What had happened tonight, and what burdens did he carry that had stolen the light from his eyes—the light so perfectly captured in the photo on his bookshelf?

NINE

I can live alone, if self-respect, and circumstances require me so to do. I need not sell my soul to buy bliss. I have an inward treasure born with me, which can keep me alive if all extraneous delights should be withheld, or offered only at a price I cannot afford to give.

The next several evenings, I took Flo out to play with Emily. Her enthusiasm for the dog and the bond between them seemed to increase daily. Roger complied with Emily's wishes to be outside, but he still never joined us. I'd sit on my lawn chair in the shade with a chocolate magazine and, you guessed it, a bit of chocolate to nibble. Emily would run with the dog and roll in the grass, and then hug Flo around the neck. "I love you, Flo," she'd repeat several times. That was all fine, but Flo was getting the exercise and I wasn't. Chocolate plus no exercise equals hips.

Even though I don't work Saturday mornings, I got up early that Saturday to go into the shop. We don't open until 10:00, but I had noticed during the week that the shop needed some good scrubbing, and today seemed a good day to do it. Carmen and Cricket came in much earlier to get ready for the day.

Even before I opened the door, I could smell cacao beans roasting. *Yum.* As I walked through the door, I heard Cricket hiccup. That poor girl!

Cricket's real name is Sarah, and she's had her hiccupping problem since early childhood. According to her story, when she was in elementary school, she heard an announcement over the PA system asking "Sarah" to report to the office. When she arrived, four other girls had come too. Soon the principal appeared, holding up a lunch pail with a long strip of masking tape stuck to the bottom with the name "Sarah" scribbled across it. One of the girls claimed it, but before they all went back to class, the principal said, "We can't have five girls named Sarah in such a small school. You each need to pick a nickname."

Immediately following his comment, Cricket squeaked out a hiccup.

"You sound like a cricket," the principal said.

The name stuck.

Carmen greeted me as I filled the cleaning bucket with soapy water. "I wish you could have been at our hula program last night, Janie, and saved me from this Viking guy."

"A sewing machine salesman?" I asked, then glanced over at Cricket, who rolled her eyes and then hiccupped.

"No, he's some guy from Norway. We did a show for the Kiwanis Club. I walked out of our dressing room and there he was, waiting for me! He asked if he could buy me a drink. I was so embarrassed!"

"Why?" I carried the bucket past her into the shop. "I think it would be a compliment."

"The other girls came out right behind me and heard him try to hit on me." She huffed. "They know I don't date redheads. My dear departed husband was a redhead." She played with her own natural auburn braid. "We made quite a striking pair. And after he died, to honor him, I said, 'No more reds.'"

Cricket rolled her eyes again and hiccupped.

"I thought you didn't drink," I said, ringing out the rag.

"I don't," replied Carmen, "but I would have been happy with a Coke."

"So what did you do?"

"I told him if he'd dye his hair blond, I'd go out with him. He followed me through the lobby and asked me again if I'd like to have a drink with him. I said no again. Isn't 'no' the same in every language?" Carmen frowned as she looked at me and then Cricket.

"In German, no is 'nein,'" Cricket said, "or something like that." *Hiccup.*

"I don't know. He followed me out to my car and asked for my phone number. I gave it to him, but told him there was no use in calling because I don't date redheads. Then I got in and drove away."

I laughed as I scrubbed the counter. "I bet you broke his heart!"

"I've got to keep my commitment."

"Last time it was a millionaire from Mexico," Cricket said. *Hiccup.* "He didn't have red hair."

"Yeah," Carmen said, turning to her, "but he said he wanted me to see his etchings in his apartment."

I turned away and snickered.

"Why are you laughing, Janie? I dated an artist once and swore I never would again. They're way too temperamental."

"Do you believe he really had etchings?" I asked.

"He wouldn't lie to me, would he?"

Cricket rolled her eyes again. "Think about it, Mom. As naive as you are about men and their pickup lines, I'm surprised you haven't got yourself in bigger trouble."

Linc walked in and let the back door slam. "What's happening?" he said, obviously in a fine mood.

"I'm cleaning." I held up my rag as evidence. "What are you doing here on a Saturday? You know we don't do deliveries today."

"I have a date." He vaulted onto the counter to sit. "And I'm meeting her here in" —he looked at his watch— "five minutes. She's got some business downtown, and then we're going to walk on the bridge, and then play in the sprinklers at the park."

Cricket laughed. "The sprinklers are for toddlers. Duh!" *Hiccup.*

"Well, I feel like a kid again! I feel all jittery inside! Today—"

"Lincoln Rockefeller Gates, I think you are in love." I laughed. "I've never seen you in such a mood."

He shook his head. "I'm not in love but I just might let myself go there with Jackie. This girl is different, you know? She's as smooth as glass. She's just so, well, happy, and it makes me happy to be with her."

I dropped my rag into the bucket and stood straight. "Is this the religious fanatic you were telling me about who did your hair?"

"Yeah, that's the one. She's so clean, she squeaks." He smiled at his own joke. "She hasn't even let me kiss her yet." He raised his eyebrows.

The door opened and we all turned to watch an attractive, petite black girl walk in. Linc was right. She radiated happiness. Her smile lit up the room, and she was dressed in jeans and a pink sweater. A few natural curls fell around her face, and the rest of her hair was pulled back in a ponytail.

Linc jumped down from the counter. "Ya'll, this is Jackie."

Jackie waved and smiled at us. Linc slid across the countertop to stand beside her. "This is where I work and these are some of the sweet ladies I work with." He told her our names.

"Wow! What a cool shop. It's decorated so nice." Jackie looked around at the pictures of chocolate creations on the wall. "It's great to meet you all. Linc has told me so much about the shop, and about each of you."

He took her hand. "See you ladies later," he said to us. They walked out hand in hand as the bell chimed.

I must have left my mouth hanging open because Carmen reached over and closed it.

"Yep. In love," she said. "And to think she has that much power without even kissing him."

At that, Cricket hiccupped.

TEN

Even for me life had its gleams of sunshine.

Each Sunday, you could find me sitting in the same inconspicuous spot on the right side of the chapel. Taylor Palms is less than a block from the chapel. I had a bad habit of waiting until the last minute to arrive at church, and I usually walked in as the bishop stood to welcome the congregation. That I arrived a few minutes early one Sunday surprised me. Then Roger and Emily came in and sat behind me—another good surprise.

Emily leaned forward to ask quietly, "Janie, where's Flo?"

I turned around. "She's home."

"Why didn't she come with you?"

I glanced at Roger, who tried not to smile. Then I answered Emily as seriously as I could. "Because dogs don't come to church, only people."

Her beautiful blue eyes got larger and her eyebrows flew

up. "Who's playing with her?"

"Nobody. She's in the backyard and probably barking at everyone who walks by."

She turned to Roger. "Can I sit with Janie, Daddy?" Before I knew it, she was on my pew, tightly clutching a child's baptism book. Her dress matched the blue of her eyes and had a frocked princess waist, and she wore white-lace-trimmed socks with black baby-doll shoes. The meeting began and she sat quietly. I squirmed uncomfortably, knowing Roger was directly behind me.

It's amazing what goes through your head when the man you are infatuated with is sitting behind you. You're afraid to move too much, yet you're afraid of sitting like stone. You have to sit perfectly straight. You worry about dandruff flakes. You hope you remembered to pull your dress zipper all the way up. Your head starts itching, even though you just washed your hair, and you learn how hard it is not to scratch, and you can't because he will think you have lice.

Misery!

During the closing prayer, I scratched, hoping Roger's eyes were closed. "Amen!" I stood and turned around. "Thanks for letting Emily sit with me," I said cheerfully. "I can take her to Primary if you want."

Roger agreed. Before Emily and I headed to the Primary room, Brother Toone came up to Roger and introduced himself. Knowing Roger was in good hands, I took Emily's hand and we slipped away down the hall.

Since the Primary was small, I knew Emily would get the attention she needed. I found the CTR-4 teacher, Sister Jones, and introduced her to Emily. Emily seemed pleased to join the other children, so as the opening song began, I slipped out the door and back to the chapel to the Gospel Doctrine class.

This time, I sat behind Roger and wondered if he squirmed.

Okay, bear with me as I divulge a few more sappy thoughts. There is something romantic about parting with the man you love to go to Relief Society, knowing he is going to priesthood meeting. You are both having the same gospel lesson, learning the same concepts. There's a unity between you even though you are apart. You are growing together in the gospel.

Completely submerged in this thought, I just knew things would change now between Roger and me—that our relationship would become closer, and that his wounds would heal so his heart could love again. The last hour ended, and my head was filled with these romantic notions as I went looking for the man I loved and his precious daughter.

I passed the foyer, intending to go down the hall to find Sister Jones's classroom. But through the glass door that led to the parking lot, I saw the young woman who had come into the shop looking for Roger, standing in the shade of the entry. I stopped abruptly and stared. The woman wore jeans and another plunging neckline, but her hair now looked clean as if it had made that desperately needed rendezvous with a bottle of shampoo. She leaned against the wall with one high-heeled foot up behind her, and a large handbag hung from her shoulder. The woman appeared to carefully scrutinize each person who left the building.

I hurried into the chapel, where the elder's quorum meeting had just dismissed and the men were filing out. Roger and the quorum president stood talking in the back of the chapel.

"Roger?" I interrupted as inconspicuously as possible. "Uh, I need you."

Several men turned to look at me and then at Roger, and smiles crept across their faces. I smiled back.

"Please, excuse us Brother Toone," I said and pulled on Roger's arm for him to follow.

All heads turned to watch us leave the chapel. We didn't walk into the foyer—just far enough into the hall to see the girl.

"That woman," I said, pointing guardedly toward the door, "came into the shop looking for you about two weeks ago. She claimed she was your sister."

The ward busybody, Sister Lilly, passed us at that moment, looking at me with raised eyebrows.

Roger watched the woman who stood outside. "I don't know who she is, and she is not my sister. I—" As the woman turned, he stopped mid-sentence, took my arm, and hurried me back into the chapel.

"What is it?" I asked, noticing that the color had drained from his handsome face. I pulled him over to sit on the back pew. "Who is she?"

"She's—" He rubbed his forehead. "I can't let her see me, but if she does . . ." He looked around the chapel. "Will you please take Emily home?" He pulled out his cell phone and opened a new contact window, then pushed the phone into my hand. "Put your number in here so I can call you."

This wasn't quite the moment I had always dreamed of when he would finally ask me for my phone number. But in an odd way, the previously fantasized Relief Society/priesthood unity had just clicked for Roger and me.

"I'll be glad to keep Emily," I declared as I punched in my cell number. "I'll need to take her with me to my sister's for dinner. But please tell me what's going on!"

He stood and took his phone, then took hold of my hand. "I'll have to explain later. Thanks for helping me out again." He turned, left the chapel, and quickly headed out the foyer on the opposite side of the chapel.

ELEVEN

This was the point—this was where the nerve was touched and teased—this was where the fever was sustained and fed: she could not charm him.

I stood there dumbfounded, staring at my hand. He actually had held it! Yes, he held it very briefly, the way a brother would grasp his sister's hand in encouragement, but it wasn't merely a handshake. He voluntarily touched me! My breathing stopped, my heart, my brain—and not until he was gone did my senses return.

As if I had just won a million dollars, I floated out of the chapel. I passed the foyer and saw the strange woman still standing outside the door. My happy mood dissipated. I hurried down the hall and found Sister Jones and Emily waiting in a classroom doorway.

"We learned that we lived with Heavenly Father before we were borned," Emily told me as she pointed to the paper crown on her head that read, "I am a child of God."

I glanced uneasily back up the hall as Sister Jones added,

"She was wonderful in class. Knew all the answers, too."

Emily nodded in agreement. I thanked the teacher and took Emily's hand and started away from the foyer, hoping the stranger wouldn't see me, especially with Roger's child. Did the woman also have a picture of Emily? Not many little girls in the ward had wild, curly blond hair, so the child holding my hand wouldn't be hard to pick out in a crowd.

"Where's Daddy?" Emily asked.

"He's coming later," I said, not wanting to explain at that moment. We walked across the cultural hall, exited out the west foyer, and hurried to the street. I didn't see anyone who looked out of place, but I practically pushed Emily down the sidewalk. I glanced over my shoulder several times before we turned the corner into our courtyard. Even then, I didn't feel safe. I had to protect Emily.

Seeing us over the wall, Flo barked. I couldn't get my key out of my scripture bag fast enough, imagining danger on our heels. I looked around but saw no one. After I got the door to my cottage open, I pushed Emily through.

She ran to the patio window. "Flo is out there!" she squealed.

I opened the door and the canine bounded in. She went right to Emily and sat calmly to let the little girl hug her.

"This scene is indeed heart warming, but we need to leave." I looked at Emily's frilly dress, and, remembering the key Roger gave me for emergencies, wondered if I should take the time to get some clothes for her to change into. *What if the woman comes? What if she knows where Roger lives?* Feeling an urgency to leave the premises, I decided against the change of clothes. Kylee's daughters would certainly have something for Emily to wear.

"Where are we going?" Emily asked cheerily.

"To play with my nieces. They are a lot of fun and will love you to visit." I grabbed the leash and quickly led Emily and Flo to my car. I opened the back door and remembered Arizona's child safety laws and that I had no booster chair. Flo jumped in and sat on the seat. Emily followed and I only hesitated a moment before I buckled her in with the seatbelt.

"Be very good and stay in the seat. Be very calm so that Flo will be calm too. Sometimes she gets nervous and jumps around." Actually, Flo behaved very well in the car; I just had no idea how Emily would react. The little girl smiled and put her arm around Flo.

"We will be fine. Right, Flo?" she said to the dog.

All the way to Kylee's house, I ran the day's events over in my mind. *Who is this woman who is looking for Roger? Is she Winnie Wentworth?* She definitely wasn't the happy woman in the photo with Roger. I remembered the shock on Roger's face, his tense hands when he handed me his cell phone, the abrupt manner in which he turned and left the chapel. I could make no sense of any of it.

Kylee's daughters took Emily under their wing as soon as she walked through the door. And so much for a change of clothes—I saw Emily in several different outfits throughout the evening. To Whitney and Jaxlynn, Kylee's daughters who are first- and third-graders, Emily was more of a doll to them with her tumbling curls and rosy, round face. Flo also became part of the dress-up party, first appearing in a hat, then with a scarf. She followed the girls around and I knew she was having the time of her life. Kylee's son Paul, the oldest, protested that dressing up was silly, but soon came out fully clad in a pirate costume, waving a plastic sword.

"And then he left with no explanation," I told Kylee as we cleaned up after dinner. "I've never been a part of something so mysterious before." I picked up my cell phone and looked at it. "Oh, I wish this thing would ring!"

Riiiiinng!

I fumbled to open the phone. "Hello?"

"This is Roger. Where are you?"

"I'm at my sister's. Emily is with me. Where are you?"

"At the police station. I take it you got away from the church all right."

"Yes, but—"

"How is Emily?"

"She's fine, but—"

"Listen, Janie. I won't be going back to my house tonight. I'll be by to get Emily in a few minutes. Tell me where your sister lives."

Confused, I tried to think of "rights" and "lefts" and addresses, but it all came out jumbled. Kylee took the phone and calmly gave directions. Then she clicked off the phone. "He's on his way."

I didn't know what to say or do. "I'm scared," I confessed. "What is this all about?"

There was no use for Kylee and me to try to figure out the mystery. It was clear that there was much more to this incident than we could imagine, and that the woman's inquiries were only the greens of the carrot.

At last the doorbell rang. Looking like a costume party, Whitney, Jaxlynn, Emily, and Flo beat me to the door and opened it. Roger stood there looking tense but as attractive as ever. I wanted to leap into his arms, but Emily beat me to it.

He swooped the tiny girl up and hugged her. "Hi, princess, I've missed you. I'm so glad you're all right." She kissed his cheek, and then the three girls and a deer—for now Flo wore antlers—ran up the stairs again.

Roger came into the house without being asked and closed the door. "Don't worry. I parked around the corner." He looked exhausted.

"What's going on?"

"The police followed me back to the church, but the woman was gone."

"Who is she?" I asked. "Why did you have to leave?"

Roger opened his mouth to answer, but just then Kylee joined us in the entry. I introduced them.

"Won't you come in and have something to eat?" Kylee asked. "You look hungry."

He didn't respond immediately, so I took his arm and led him into the kitchen and sat him on a stool at the counter. Kylee set to work filling a plate and warming the food.

"Daddy!" Emily shouted as she ran into the kitchen wearing a pumpkin costume. "Look at me!"

"You look very—orange." He took her up into his arms again and buried his face in her wild curls. She wiggled away and ran off with the girls again, oblivious of her father's distress.

Kylee and I exchanged glances. What kind of trouble was Roger in?

She put the plate of food in front of him. As he started eating, there was an awkward silence, so Kylee started rambling on about the boys in her Primary class and the funny things they had done that day. Roger chuckled politely, and when he had eaten every morsel, he thanked her for the dinner.

"Emily and I need to be leaving." He stood.

"If you aren't going back to Taylor Palms, where will you stay tonight?"

He shrugged. "My mother's, maybe."

"Maybe?"

"My brother's, maybe, or a hotel." He paused, obviously trying to figure things out. "I guess I won't go to Mom's. She'll try to get involved, and that's the last thing I need."

"Stay here with us," Kylee invited. "My husband will be back from his Scout committee meeting soon. You can sleep on the hide-a-bed in the den, and Emily can sleep upstairs with the girls."

"I couldn't impose on you like that."

"Nonsense."

Roger looked from Kylee to Janie. "You ladies have been so good. You know nothing about me, yet you're willing to take me in—a perfect stranger."

"I've been living next door to you for almost two weeks, so you aren't a stranger." I said. *And in love with you for much, much longer than that.*

"And you've been coming to our shop all these months and you haven't mugged us yet."

Kylee and I thought that was funny, but Roger just looked at us.

"You are too kind," he finally said quietly.

"Then it's all settled," Kylee said. "I'll prepare the bed for you."

She left Roger and I standing alone in the kitchen. He sheepishly looked at me. "Does your sister always take in strays?"

I put my hand on his arm. "Only when they have an adorable four-year-old."

He smiled briefly, but then the worry returned to dominate his dark eyes.

At that moment the girls came running in, laughing and squealing, led by their pirate captain. Flo, wearing a tutu around her middle, made up the rear. They ran through the kitchen and into the family room, then bounced on the couch and giggled hysterically. Pirates and ballet dancers! So much for a quiet Sabbath.

"I'm sorry about what has happened today. You've been so good to take Emily, and I can't thank your family enough for taking us in. I'll talk to the police again tomorrow about keeping an eye on my apartment so I can go home. I want Emily to have some stability instead of camping out at other people's houses every night."

"Is that what you did before moving into Taylor Palms?"

"Practically. We've had a rough go of it." He didn't offer more.

"Well, then. I hope you're able to tell me about it soon." I had already hinted sufficiently that I wanted to know the details.

"I don't want to drag you into my problems. If I don't tell you, then you can honestly say you don't know anything if anyone comes snooping around the apartment."

"Anyone? You mean it's not just that woman?"

"No, it isn't just her." The tone of his voice told me I was pushing him too far. He stepped a few feet away, my heart following him.

We watched the girls frolicking in the family room. "Let's go outside," Roger said after a few minutes.

I led him to the front door and opened it. The mid-October night air was cool and refreshing. We walked several feet from the porch and I waited for him to speak.

"It has to do with a crime that I . . . was a witness to . . . after the fact. I saw three people—the girl at the church, one man named Jack who is now in jail, and one man who is still on the loose. When the girl made the mistake of coming to Jack's trial, I identified her to the prosecutor and they arrested her on the spot. That was after she heard my testimony on the stand.

"She spent time in jail, but only three months because she maintained—and Jack supported her claim—that she was an innocent bystander. I actually believe her. Anyway, they notified me when she was released from jail.

"I don't know how she found me at the church. I've kept low for a year now. That's why Emily and I moved near the temple. A lower-rent district seemed the perfect place for us to hide."

"Why?" I asked, then sighed. "I don't know anything about you, Roger, except you have an adorable daughter and you buy a lot of chocolate." He didn't smile, so I added, "And that you are in trouble."

"The less you know, the better. I've already told you more than I should have."

"What was the crime?"

He looked far down the quiet street and rubbed his forehead. I concluded that he wasn't planning to answer, yet he did.

"Murder."

TWELVE

Here then I was . . . fastened into one of its mystic cells; night around me; a pale and bloody spectacle under my eyes and hands; a murderer hardly separated from me by a single door: yes—that was appalling.

Murder! I nearly went into shock at the word, and Roger took my arm as if he thought I would collapse onto the sidewalk. As he helped me back to Kylee's front door, he asked me to go by his apartment and put some of Emily's clothes in a bag. That way, he explained, when he came by early in the morning, he could grab the bag and whatever else he needed for the day, or two days, or three—as long as it took until he felt safe to go home again. He would take Emily to her usual private-home day care before going to his office.

With all the thoughts and worries flitting through my mind, I'm not sure how I managed to drive Flo and myself home to our cottage, but we made it.

I pulled into my parking space and noticed that the lights were on in Sister Carter's apartment. She must have returned from Utah sometime that day. Flo and I got out of the car, and Sister Carter opened her door as we passed.

"Hello, Janie. You're out late tonight." Sister Carter had always showed interest in my life. She was a short woman with white curly hair—the perfect grandmother with a sweet disposition. Naturally, I stopped to talk.

"Yes. I went to Kylee's for the evening. I hope you had a good time in Salt Lake."

"Wonderful, as usual. I got back this morning, too late to attend church, and I was so exhausted. I see a new tenant has moved into number 2."

"Yes. His name is Roger Wentworth. He has a four-year-old daughter."

"A young woman came by this morning while I was unpacking my car, asking about the apartment."

"A woman?" I asked, fearing the worst.

"Yes. I told her I thought someone had moved in. Then she was very pushy about finding the person. I suggested she go to the meetinghouse and see if she could find you. I assumed the new person in the apartment was a friend of our landlady and also LDS, and had gone to church with you."

"Well, he is LDS."

"Did the young woman find you then? She seemed awfully determined."

"Somehow I missed her." *Thank goodness!*

We said good night and Sister Carter closed the door. Flo and I went into our apartment and I got a few grocery bags for Emily's clothes. Flo settled in the shadows on the grass as I went to Roger's alone. On Roger's doorstep, I paused to look at the emergency key. I pressed it to my heart and allowed myself a brief sappy-romance moment, thinking how he had entrusted me with it. *If I were a schoolgirl,*

I thought, *I might even wear the key on a chain around my neck.*

Okay, enough of this silliness. I wasn't a schoolgirl and I didn't have a chain. This was an *emergency*, and this was an *emergency key*. Nothing more. I unlocked the door, then closed it behind me, went to Emily's room, and opened the drawers. Her clothes were sorted in neat, folded piles. I pulled out all the underwear and put them in a bag. I added pants and shirts, then filled another grocery bag. I didn't know how many clothes to put in, but I figured too many was better than not enough. I left the bags on the couch and opened the door.

There stood the woman with the plunging neckline. "Hello," she said. "Do you live here?"

I stepped back. "I—do—" I would have said "over there" and pointed across the way, but she cut me off.

"And the man, who is he to you?" she demanded.

"He's . . . just a friend."

Flo left the shadows and came quietly to stand behind the woman. I looked at the dog, and when the woman turned to follow my gaze, she jumped almost a foot off the ground. She grabbed at the neckline of her blouse and whimpered.

When she gained her composure, she asked, "Is this your bodyguard?"

"She's a friend."

"You have a lot of friends." She didn't take her eyes off Flo. "Please, tell your man friend I only want to talk with him. No harm will come. I just have something to say. And tell him to quit hiding. I will find him anyway. Tell him, okay?"

"I will."

The woman turned on her heels and only glanced back once toward Flo, probably to make sure she wasn't being followed, before entering the street. A taller form joined her, that of a man, no doubt. They disappeared down the street together and into the night.

You might wonder if at that moment I was scared. No brainer! Even though I did have a 120-pound bodyguard, this woman was mixed up in a murder that Roger witnessed. The man was probably the one Roger referred to as on-the-loose. I had no idea what to expect.

I waited about a minute to make sure the woman had gone before I quietly slipped back to my apartment, Flo following me. Hopefully, the woman and her friend wouldn't backtrack and wait for Roger to come home. I called him and told him what had happened.

After a long moment, Roger spoke. "We're dealing with murderers here, so this can't be ignored. I'll call the police right now."

THIRTEEN

Do you feel as if you should sleep, Miss?" asked Bessie, rather softly.

Scarcely dared I answer her; for I feared the next sentence might be rough. "I will try."

Not until the police agreed to pay particular attention to our apartment complex on their rounds did Roger and Emily come back home. If Florentine hadn't been with me, I may have gone to Kylee's to stay overnight until they returned. Sister Carter was still home, so at least I wasn't completely alone. For the next several nights, I spent more time tossing and turning than I did sleeping.

Often, a police car parked on Kimball or LeSueur Street. Other than their presence, life seemed normal for a whole week. Roger came in and ordered a chocolate rose for Winnie, as usual, and took an elephant home for Emily. To my dismay, the relationship that I hoped would blossom was going nowhere.

How do you eat an elephant? One nibble at a time. How do you get a man to fall in love with you? I have absolutely no idea. My cheerfulness, my smile, and my friendliness were clearly ineffective. Each morning, I went to work, and each evening I came home and watched Flo and Emily play together on the courtyard grass. Each time, Roger stayed in his apartment doing paperwork. I figured when he was ready to talk to me, he'd come out of hiding.

A week after the woman showed up at our apartment complex, the police stopped parking nearby. I still caught daily glimpses of them driving by and figured that was their way of keeping their promise to Roger. But it seemed that the police's attention to Roger's safety had waned, and that was probably what the murderer was banking on.

Roger remained aloof the following week too, and though he and Emily and I sat on the same pew at church, he and I sat miles apart. Actually, it was about eight feet, with Emily between us. The three of us walked home together, which was only around the corner. I'm sure it all spurred a few ward members' tongues to wagging and their minds to speculating.

One day when I came home, I found Roger sitting on the lawn and Emily wearing a dress with a full skirt, twirling and twirling. When she saw me, she said, "Look at me, Janie!"

"Beautiful! You look like a princess." I walked to my cottage door to free Flo from confinement. She bounded out in joy, looking a bit like a miniature bronco. Soon she and Emily sat on the grass together.

"Don't get your dress dirty, babe." Roger appeared more relaxed than I'd seen him in weeks.

I pulled my lawn chair closer to him and sat.

He said, "Please, thank Kylee again for taking Emily and me in last Sunday night."

"Of course. She said you left so early Monday morning that Jim didn't get to meet you."

Roger smiled. "I hated to interrupt their morning routine, and I had to be to work early anyway."

He surprised me by staying to talk with me instead of slipping off into his apartment, and I didn't want to say anything that might make him decide to leave.

"Do you enjoy being an attorney?" I asked. That seemed safe enough.

He sighed heavily. "I went to law school because my parents wanted me to. Practically from the moment of my birth, I knew law was what they wanted for me. Anytime I had another interest, or got involved in other activities, my mother scolded me. 'You've got to get good grades,' she'd say. 'Get in there and study! You have to get into law school.'" Roger chuckled and shook his head. "I have a very painful memory of the time I told my mother I was writing a novel."

"A novel? How cool!"

From the look on his face, he clearly didn't share my joy. "She searched for the manuscript. I'm sure she would have destroyed it if she had found it. I still have it and work on it from time to time."

"You have the manuscript? I'd love to see it."

He gazed up at me uncertainly. "Do you promise not to be too critical?"

"I promise." I raised my palm. "And I also promise not to show it to your mother." I thought that was funny.

He stood, brushed the debris from his pants, and disappeared into his apartment. Emily and Flo still sat together quietly on the grass, Emily singing softly. In a few moments, Roger returned with a three-ring notebook in hand. He sat again and opened the cover. The title page read *The Sailor's Bride.*

"It needs a more enticing title. But I hear publishers choose their own titles anyway."

"*The Sailor's Bride* is a wonderful title," I assured him.

"When the sailor is a boy, he flees his domineering father's home and takes a position on a ship set for the Pacific islands. They stop for a furlough on a tropical island, where he falls in love with a young and beautiful native girl. They marry, but now he is torn between his love for her and his love for the sea. He sets out to sea and misses his bride. He stays on the island and misses the sea—torn between two worlds, two loves. It doesn't have an adequate ending yet. Somebody must die to end the conflict."

"Can't he just stay home with her?"

"And be tormented by the sea? It is a never-ending story."

I saw his point. "May I read it?"

He laughed. "No one has ever read it. No, I take that back. Winnie has read it."

Winnie! He finally said her name outside of the shop.

"Did she like it?"

He smiled, and if I had been wearing socks, they would've been knocked off. "Oh, yes. She raved about everything I did. She was my biggest fan before—" He seemed to get lost in his thoughts.

At last, my opportunity to ask. "Who is Win—"

"Daddy!" Emily came running to us. "Can we go with Flo and Janie on their walk tonight? I promised Flo I would."

I looked up to see Flo stretched out to her maximum length on the grass, her tail wagging violently. Roger studied Emily's anxious face. "I guess, sweetheart. Let's get you out of this dress and into shorts and we'll go."

What a shock! Roger Wentworth—the make-himself-scarce RW—had finally consented to taking a walk with his daughter and her favorite canine. I would go along to hold tight to the leash.

Soon we humans had changed into suitable clothing, and the three of us set out with Flo. Roger either kept far ahead of me with Emily or lagged behind, but he never walked at my side. We chatted about how beautiful the temple grounds were and how good it was to see so many temple patrons coming and going, but we spent most of our time answering Emily's questions about everything she saw.

When we returned to Taylor Palms, Roger opened the narrow front gate. Emily went through first, then Flo. Roger placed his hand gently on my back to guide me through as he followed. I enjoyed the brief, gentle touch and the thought of him walking so closely behind me.

"Hello, Roger!"

I looked up to see an older woman sitting in my lawn chair. Roger left me and walked over to her.

"Hello, Mother."

"Grandma!" Emily exclaimed and ran into the woman's arms.

I remembered her as the woman who had waited with Emily outside the temple on the evening I saw Roger there. She hugged the child, then stood. She wore a pantsuit of black and yellow, with matching purse and shoes. Her hair and makeup looked as if she had just walked out of a beauty salon. Roger gave her a brief hug and turned to introduce us. His mother stared at me with a cold, stony expression.

"Hello," I greeted, trying to act as if I hadn't noticed the daggers she had sent my direction.

Without responding, she turned to Roger. "We need to talk."

He nodded goodbye to me as Emily took the woman's hand and pulled her toward their apartment.

Disappointed that my evening with Roger and Emily had ended, I turned and led Flo to my door. As I unlocked it, I heard Roger's mother say, "I've just come from visiting Winnie . . ."

FOURTEEN

"To speak truth, sir, I don't understand you at all: I cannot keep up the conversation, because it has got out of my depth . . ."

"Justly thought; rightly said, Miss Eyre; and, at this moment, I am paving hell with energy."

oger came into the shop the following Tuesday. Since Halloween was only a few days away, he chose for Emily a witch on a flying broomstick across a full moon. After I handed Roger his box and receipt, I gave him one of the Superdads I had on display.

"This is just a gift from one neighbor to another." I blushed from ear to ear, wondering if Roger noticed that Superdad's face resembled his own.

He hardly looked at the piece. I knew that he knew that I knew I was flirting (did you follow that?), trying to take some sort of step to push along our romance. He still didn't take the bait.

"You're one of the first to see it," I informed him.

"Thank you, neighbor." He picked it up rather indifferently and started to leave.

"I'm almost done with your novel. You're a good writer! When I'm done, we can talk about it, if you'd like. I've made a few notes and circled some typos I found. I hope you don't mind."

"Not at all. I can use all the help I can get," Roger said. I hoped he would loosen up so we could have a real conversation, but he followed with, "I'd rather you just give it to me with your written comments."

He hardly glanced at me again before he left, leaving me dumbfounded, heartbroken, and confused. All I could imagine was that his mother had given him the word to distance himself from me. But why? Did she think I wasn't good enough—pretty and rich enough—for him?

I sulked all day. I had a right to, since Roger clearly had given me the brush-off.

Willa arrived in the afternoon and I went into the back of the shop to work. I just didn't feel like putting on a smile and acting cheery for customers.

Between customers, Willa stood in the doorway to talk with me. "What do you know about ambulances?"

An odd question. "Is that what you're into now?" I asked. "What happened to fire eating?"

"I'm still doing that."

"And bungee jumping?"

"That too, but now I'm thinking of driving an ambulance."

I thought for a moment. "Well, I know it's a dangerous job. People get killed in collisions with ambulances. I always thought that was ironic—you're rushing people to the hospital to save their lives and you lose yours because someone didn't see you rushing to save lives."

Willa stared at me for a few seconds, probably trying to make sense of the jumble, then said, "Well, I met this really cute guy who is a driver, and he thinks he can arrange for me to ride with him sometime."

I laughed in wonder at Willa and all her interests. "Best wishes, girl. Just don't enjoy it so much that you leave the shop. We really like you here."

Willa smiled. The bell rang and she left to wait on the customer.

Again, Linc didn't have time to deliver the box to North Mesa. His aunt was ill and he needed to take his mother to see her. To use the few minutes before he would leave, I put him to work sorting cacao beans, while I poured chocolate into molds.

I asked about Jackie. "Have you kissed her yet?"

"No score," he answered with disappointment in his voice. "She says kissing is off limits, but that when she's good and ready, she'll kiss me. It amazes me." He smiled to himself as he picked out rocks and debris. "Even though her lips are taboo, I can't keep away. I gotta be with her all the time."

"Do you like her because she's playing hard to get?"

"I don't think that's it." He tossed a handful of rocks into the trash. "She treats me cool, even calls me her boyfriend." He thought for a moment. "And I think her brain is right on track, because we can still have fun without all that high-pressure stuff. Most girls would expect more than kissing by now, if you know what I mean, and it usually ruins a relationship."

He went on, talking about Jackie's talents and how fun she was. I listened in amazement and realized how much Linc had matured since meeting this fine young woman.

"Now I'm certain you're in love," I said with a grin when he finished.

Jackie's different, all right. Says she'll never live with a guy until she's hitched." He put a pile of sorted beans into a large bowl. "I couldn't have found a girl like her if I had searched this entire planet." He pulled out his cell phone, glanced at the time, and headed toward the door. "Oh, man! I'd better get goin' if I'm gonna pick up Mama in time!"

I drove out to the Val Vista mansion myself. When I arrived, the routine was the same as the week before. I announced myself at the intercom and the gate opened. In spite of its well-kept green lawns and the beauty of the mansion house, I wondered at the mystery of the place.

The same Asian woman answered the door, wearing a cheerful smile. I handed her the clipboard to sign. Behind her, a tall woman cautiously crept into the hallway. Her long, dark hair hug loosely over her shoulders, and the light blue, flowing pantsuit she wore could not hide her slender figure.

The nurse spoke to her without turning around. "Winnie, another rose has arrived for you from the chocolate shop."

Smiling, Winnie came closer. She was the same young woman I had seen in the photo in Roger's living room. There was an unwell, haunting look in her eyes, but her face was beautiful.

I handed Winnie the box and she hugged it to her chest. "Thank you," she said so quietly that I almost didn't hear her. "What is your name?"

"Janie."

"Janie." Winnie repeated softly and released the box to look at it. "Your name is here," she said, smoothing her hand over my signature.

"Yes. I make the chocolate."

"I will remember," she said in a childlike tone.

A low-pitched buzzing came from a metal box labeled "Front Gate" on the hall table. We each turned to look at it. Grace pushed a flashing button and spoke into the box. "May I help you?"

The speakerphone blared a woman's voice. "Is this the

Wentworth residence?"

"Yes."

"I'm the caseworker assigned to Winifred Wentworth. I wrote down the wrong phone number, or I would have called ahead. Is this a convenient time to visit and see how Winifred is doing?"

Grace sighed and looked at her watch. "I guess we can give you a few minutes." She pushed another button on the box—I assumed it was to open the gate—and then guided Winnie to sit on a white chair near the entrance. "Oh, how I hate to interrupt Winifred's routine!"

Feeling awkward, I stepped back and fumbled for the doorknob. "I, uh, hope you have a lovely day. Goodbye."

"Goodbye," Winnie whispered, holding the box carefully on her lap.

"Goodbye," Grace said.

I closed the door behind me and went to my car. The caseworker had parked her car behind mine. Her blonde hair had fallen across her face as she looked through an accordion file. I got into my car and followed the circular drive. The woman still sat in her car as I drove through the gate.

I met Winnie! Now I could go back to my shop and tell the others about the face that went along with the name. When Roger mentioned Winnie, I would know whom he spoke of.

And what a beautiful house! Everything about it was impressive—the neatness of the white interior, the quiet solitude, the immaculate lawns. *A haven in the city limits.*

Who is Winnie to Roger? I wondered. *She's clearly not his white-haired old mother. Maybe she's a sister.* My gut feeling was that she was his wife, but since they didn't live together and he didn't wear a ring, they were clearly either divorced or separated. A sense of guilt swept over me for hoping the first.

FIFTEEN

Well, you too have power over me, and may injure me: yet I dare not show you where I am vulnerable, lest, faithful and friendly as you are, you should transfix me at once.

By Thursday, our sales skyrocketed. We had used every Halloween mold we could find in our supplies. I came into the shop much earlier than usual to try to catch up and found Carmen chanting while stirring the chocolate, "'Double, double, toil and trouble, Fire burn, and caldron bubble.'"

"Getting in the Halloween mood?" I asked.

"Just quoting a little Shakespeare." She turned off our large mixing machine.

"I didn't know you were so cultured."

"Of course I am. I'm a hula dancer. That's extremely cultured." In all seriousness, she started swaying across the room and singing, "I'm a little hula hula baby from the land of Waikiki."

"That's it!"

"What?" she asked, pulling a spoon from a drawer.

"A mold I haven't thought of yet—a hula dancer. I'll start that one as soon as Halloween is over."

Carmen dipped the spoon into the chocolate, waited a few seconds for it to cool, and then licked it—her way of testing. Then she tossed the spoon into the dishwasher. "And I will be your model."

I agreed. Carmen, though past age fifty and as pale as any "haole," had a slender figure and still looked good in a hula skirt. She wore her auburn, waist-long hair in a long braid at work, but she let it loose when dancing. Cricket also danced with the troupe when she wasn't accompanying them on the Hawaiian drums.

"That Swedish guy's been coming over." She poured cocoa powder into our largest pot, where she had started a batch of fudge.

"Isn't he Norwegian?" I asked.

"I think you're right. Well, he called me and has been coming over. I haven't yet told him where I work or he'd show up here, too."

"Did he bleach his hair? You said you wouldn't date redheads."

"I'm not dating him," she responded indignantly. "I just said he's been coming over."

I had to snicker again. It was just like Carmen not to see the difference.

The door chime rang and I stepped out to greet the customer. A very redhead, handsome man stepped up to the counter. He didn't have to say a word, for I immediately knew who he was. "Wow!" I gawked. "Uh—Carmen," I called to the kitchen.

She came out in her chocolate-smeared apron. When she saw the man, her eyes grew big, and then a delighted smile spread across her face. "Bjorn!"

"Hello, Carmen!" He looked from her, to me, then back to her again. "I won your leetle hide-and-seek game." He spoke to me. "Everythink my Carmen says is a reeddle."

Suddenly, Carmen giggled and turned on the charm. "How did you find me?"

"You said you made yummy thinks to eat, near a famous breedge, so naturally, I put eet together and here I am! But eet was not easy." After pausing to laugh heartily, he went on, "I have been searching for days. I came to take you to breakfast, or whatever you would like." His big, heart-stopping grin revealed a full mouth of straight white teeth.

Carmen took off her apron and handed it to me. "The chocolate is perfect for pouring and the fudge is in the pot." She grabbed her purse, lifted the extended counter, and left with the handsome Swede—I mean, Norwegian.

After I poured the molds and made several different-flavored batches from the fudge, I turned our Closed sign to Open, and single-handedly waited on customers until Kylee arrived. She set to work while I poured more chocolate molds. Once business slowed, Kylee went to her office and I took over waiting on customers. Whew! What a day for Carmen to leave early. *She better not make a habit of this,* I thought.

Linc arrived. "The deliveries are on the counter," I said over my shoulder as I finished up a customer order.

"All right," he said, but he didn't leave.

"What's up, Linc?"

"I've got a date with a witch tonight." He sounded cheery, but I knew something else was bothering him.

"Are you calling Jackie a witch?"

"And I'm going as a warlock with a cape and the whole

outfit. She's doing my makeup. We're going to her church for a party in the parking lot."

"Ooh! It sounds fun."

Another customer came in, so I filled her order. A few minutes later I turned around to see Linc still standing in the doorway. "Linc, I know something's wrong. What is it? Is going to Jackie's church what's bothering you?"

Clearly deep in thought, he finally looked at me. "No." Linc sat on the stool. "Some of the guys from Jackie's church have been coming over and talking with us. What they teach is really spiritual stuff. They've even got their own Bible. Oh, they believe in our Bible, but then they've got another one, too, and they read from both. They say ancient prophets in America wrote it, and it goes hand in hand with the Bible."

I listened closer. It all sounded so familiar.

"What bothers me" —he swallowed hard— "is she's going to serve a mission for her church. That's the part that's killing me. She wants to leave me for a year and a half." He fell quiet for a moment. "I'm really into her, Janie. What am I going to do?"

A mission for eighteen months? Additional scripture by ancient prophets? It all fit together now. Why hadn't I seen it before? Am I a dense Latter-day Saint, or what? To quote Cricket, *Duh!*

"Give me a minute," I said before slipping into Kylee's office and pulling a dark blue book from the shelf. She looked up to see what I was doing, and then curiously followed me into the store.

"Is this the book?" I held it out for Linc to see. Kylee peeked over my shoulder.

He looked at it and recognition filled his eyes as he took it in his hand. "You have it. The Mormons' book!"

"Kylee and I are Mormons. I mean, we're members of The Church of Jesus Christ of Latter-day Saints. Are you surprised?"

"I . . . uh . . ."

"We've had a few discussions about families being eternal. Remember?"

He nodded and stared at the book in his hands. "I knew you two were different. You've often mentioned your beliefs, but I never put it all together."

"Lately, you've pretty much focused on only one thing."

Link still sulked. "True. I wish she wasn't so dead set on this mission thing, though."

I watched him for a moment, praying for the right words. "Support her, Linc. Wait for her. Eighteen months will go fast and it will give you time to look into the Church and understand it better, and to get more schooling behind you. Jackie will be an even better person when she gets back."

"Yeah. I wish I had the faith you do. Will she still want me when she gets back?"

Kylee spoke. "That depends on you, Linc."

The door chime rang and our next customer walked in. I went to wait on her, Linc took the day's deliveries and left, and Kylee went back to her office.

SIXTEEN

"I was shut up in a room where there is a ghost till after dark."

I saw Mr. Lloyd smile and frown at the same time. "Ghost! What, you are a baby after all! You are afraid of ghosts?"

Halloween arrived on Friday and the shop bell rang all day. Projecting from the previous year's sales, I knew there were still plenty of chocolates in the display case for Tessa and Frank to sell during the downtown Halloween costume party. Armed with the rest of the unsold miniature pumpkins, witches, and black cats, I left the couple in charge and dropped by my apartment to get Flo. Then I went to the trunk-or-treat party at the church.

Judging from the number of people in the parking lot, every kid in a six-mile radius must have been there. I parked my SUV alongside the other vehicles and set up my card table. Just like me to forget a tablecloth; so much for organization. Though she watched the crowd with anticipation, Flo obediently stayed beside me. Plus I had a leash and a strong grip.

Children in costumes crowded the walkways, with or without parents tagging along. Tiny witches and ghosts hollered, "Trick or treat!" at each car trunk or table. Zombies walked the night, and pumpkins with angelic faces held out their candy buckets in hopes of yet another treat.

No sooner had I settled in than Frankenstein stopped at my table. His home-created costume featured a marshmallow glued to each side of his neck. When I stood, I noticed that he was taller than me.

"Trick or treat," he said lamely.

"I'm not giving up my special chocolate for such a wimpy request," I informed him. "Try again."

He shifted on his huge feet, which were made of boxes. "Trick or treat," he said a little louder, but with clear boredom. Maybe his mother had dragged him here and forced him to ask for candy.

Flo barked, the kid jumped, and I smirked. "She says that wasn't good enough."

"That's not a dog, it's a horse! Do you have a saddle for him?" The boy's eyes grew wide.

"No, I ride her bareback."

"Wow! It's a girl? How much does she eat?"

"How much do you weigh?" I asked.

The kid froze.

"If you can overreact about my dog, then you can say 'trick or treat' with a little more enthusiasm. Remember, this is really good chocolate."

He shifted again, and with a sigh of annoyance, he made one more attempt. I felt sorry for the guy and handed him an inch-high pumpkin. "You've got to do better next time, or no choco, kid." He took a few steps, popped the piece in his mouth, then spun around and trotted back to my table.

"Trick or treat!" he shouted with exuberance. Now that is what gladdens a chocolatier's heart and boosts her ego.

The next Halloweener, a boy in fatigues and bandages, was no more enthusiastic than Frankenstein. *What is with kids these days? Has Halloween lost its magic?* I wondered.

Next came a sweet princess in a long pink dress and a riot of curly blond hair. "Hi, Janie!" Emily said. "Trick or treat!" She bopped up and down in clear plastic slippers.

Flo, who had been lying under the table, barked and wagged her whole behind.

"Flo, you came!" she squealed, hugging the dog's head. "Do you get to trick or treat too? Where is your costume?"

"She's Scooby Doo. Can't you tell?"

Emily wagged her curls.

"Are you having fun?" I asked.

"Yes! And so is Daddy."

Hoping to see Roger, I looked up, but he was nowhere in sight. "You'd better stay here until he comes." That way I'd get to see him for sure.

"Look!" Emily stepped back and twirled to show off her elaborate dress. It flowed freely, and its green sash had been tied in a large bow. "And look at all my candy." Emily tipped her plastic jack-o'-lantern to reveal the stash within.

"Wow! You look great." I pointed toward my last customer. "Go over to that guy and teach him how to say 'trick or treat' like you do," I joked. "But come right back."

Taking me literally, Emily said, "Okay!" and bounced away. Flo started to follow.

"Flo, come back!" The Great Dane reluctantly obeyed and came to stand beside me.

I looked up and there stood Roger Wentworth, wearing jeans, a T-shirt, and a fedora. "Where's your costume?" he asked. He seemed distant as if he only spoke to me out of neighborly and churchly duty.

"I came straight from work 'cuz I figured these kids would rather have chocolate than wait for me to dress up as a witch. Who are you supposed to be?"

"Dick Tracy."

"Hmm. I see." He did look smashing, but he hardly resembled the famous detective. "I don't remember Tracy wearing jeans."

"No, but I've been in a suit all day. I thought the hat was enough." Roger stood his distance.

"I like it, but you look more like Indiana Jones."

"Okay, then I'm Indiana," he said.

Roger seemed anxious to leave, and with the detached way he treated me, I wouldn't have minded.

"Your daughter is right over there." I pointed toward a group of children around a fishing-pond curtain.

He looked up but didn't leave. A hippie stepped up to my table and I challenged her to the enthusiasm test. She passed, so I gave her a chocolate cat.

"Trick or treat!" Roger said. "There. Did I earn a chocolate too?" I handed him a witch and then noticed Sister Lilly staring at me.

Roger turned to see what had caught my eye and must have noticed the ward busybody too, because he said suddenly, "I'd better go find Emily. I promised my mother I'd bring my princess by to show off her costume."

He didn't wait for a goodbye. I watched him go to Emily, and together, they disappeared into the crowd.

Sister Lilly sat in her chair directly across the walkway from me. Every time I looked her way, she looked back even though her chair was turned to the right. It was as if there was something odd about me, like my blouse was on backwards or something. I checked. It wasn't. And if it had been, it was Halloween so I would've had an excuse. Everyone looked a little odd tonight.

More kids came to my table and I made each one speak loudly and clearly—with enthusiasm—before I gave him or her (sometimes it was hard to tell) a treat. When the crowd started to thin, I looked back at Sister Lilly. She stood by her chair, talking to a woman—a familiar woman. Then it registered in my brain: it was the same woman who kept looking for Roger! They both turned to stare at me.

I heard Sister Lilly say, "Oh, you mean Roger Wentworth?"

The strange woman turned her back to me and spoke in a lower voice. Then she turned and walked toward me. The long fringe on her low-cut, brown leather top swayed gracefully over the sleek, tight black slacks she wore over high-heeled shoes.

Before she reached me, she started talking. "Have you seen Roger Wentworth tonight? The lady across the way said he stopped at your table."

I looked around for anyone, a stranger most likely, who could have been the dark figure she had walked off with that night at Taylor Palms, but I saw no adult who looked out of place. "He came by here but said he had somewhere else to go, then left."

She looked angry. "Where did he go?"

I pointed in a direction. "Off that way."

The woman said coolly, "I assume you told him I came by your place the other night. I've tried to call on him again, but with no luck. Tell him to stop being a scaredy-cat. He doesn't need all those police cars around your place. I don't bite."

Then why do you look like a snake to me? I smiled at my own private joke and didn't bother to answer because she turned and walked away.

SEVENTEEN

"Her excesses had prematurely developed the germs of insanity. Jane, you don't like my narrative; you look almost sick—shall I defer the rest to another day?"

"No, sir, finish it now; I pity you—I do earnestly pity you."

As soon as the woman had left, I pulled out my cell phone and called Indiana, briefly telling him of my conversation with the woman.

"Thank you. I'll take care of it," he said before he hung up.

The party died out about 8:00. Flo, who had loved being around all the children and had behaved quite well, was now stretched out on the blacktop, snoozing.

I had run out of chocolate, and not wanting to wake Flo, I sat and watched the last of the crowd and enjoyed the mild evening.

Twenty-seven is an awkward age to be unmarried and a Mormon. Last Sunday our Young Adult representative, April, slapped a flyer into my hand for a dance to be held Saturday night, the night after Halloween. It was to be a big shindig at the tri-stake center.

April always treated me like a square peg where Young Adults was concerned. "I hope you can come to this," she said with a smile and a look in her eye that actually meant, "All the guys there will be way younger than you, but I'm doing my duty to let you know about the event since you're still on the list."

I've learned you should never complain about how anyone fulfills his or her calling, or you might end up with the calling. Anyway, tonight, April stopped at my table to remind me of the event in her sweet, caring way.

After the trunk or treat, I went home depressed. The party had been fun, but it didn't make up for the lack of a human male to come home to. The dance flyer stared at me from the table where I had left it. Somehow, I *had* to get my mind off Roger. Meeting eligible men seemed impossible, but I resolved reluctantly to go to that dance.

My phone rang. "Hi, Janie. This is John."

I wished I'd checked the caller ID before answering. Dread! "Hi, John. Has it been only a month since I've seen you?" (Did you catch the sarcasm?)

"Would you like to go out tomorrow night?"

I still held the dance flyer in my hand. "I'm busy. I'm going to a dance." Being the nice person I am, I added, "Would you like to come along?"

"Ha! Dancing is an abomination before the Lord! We will go to dinner instead."

"What? I didn't say—"

"I'll pick you up at 7:00."

"You must not have heard me. I'm going to the dance, so don't come to pick me up."

Now I *had* to go to the dance. Oh, bother.

The next night, even though the tri-stake center was only three blocks away and the dance didn't start until 9:00, I left my house before 7:00 just in case John still decided to come by—which is something he would have done. On my way, I went to Kylee's and sorted stray socks.

The party rocked—for the other young adults there. I danced a few times, caught up on the news with a few girls I know, said hello to April, ate a tasteless cookie, and drank a cup of Kool-Aid. The whole evening reminded me of the time I once waited for a bus in a crowded terminal, minus the cookie and drink.

And then, whom do you think I saw? Trevin Worliss, my arch-torturer from my teen years in Wickenburg. "Hi, Santa Fe! Aren't you a little old to be here?" he asked in greeting.

You'd think a returned missionary, and a man around the age of twenty-eight years, would have knocked off the rough corners of his personally by now. At first sight, I had decided to be congenial to the former creep. But now, realizing he wasn't a former, but a present, I regretted my resolve. "You are older than I am, Trevin."

He snorted. "Yeah, but it's different for guys. We look down at girls, girls look up at guys—in age, that is."

No wonder Mr. Charming wasn't married! See what gems older Mormon girls looking for a husband have to choose from? "Where am I supposed to be, if not here?" I asked.

A new song started over the PA system. "You wouldn't want to dance, would you?" I figured he was asking me to dance. That was a first.

I took a deep breath. Dancing with Trevin would be worse than spending the evening with John. "No. I think I'll go empty trash cans." As I passed him, I heard Trevin sigh with relief.

I walked through the crowd, right through the door, out to my car, drove down the road to my cottage, and parked. Before going inside to hide, I leaned my head against the steering wheel and said a silent plea that the Lord would someday bless me with a good, kind husband, without having to go to a church dance to find him.

Sunday dawned excellently. Roger and Emily sat on my bench at church—he sitting yards from me with Emily between us. I noticed heads turning and Sister Lilly's frown. Roger and I sat in silence, never speaking, never touching, and then going in opposite directions after the last "amen."

After Relief Society, I checked to see if the strange woman was waiting outside. No sign of her. I looked for Emily at Sister Jones's classroom.

"Her father came for her before the class was over. Said he needed to leave early," she told me.

I walked home alone. It was hardly a block away, but I missed the little girl who last time held my hand and skipped the whole way. Roger's car wasn't in his parking space. I put Flo in my SUV and went to Kylee's for dinner, enjoying a quiet evening with my sister. Well, as quiet as you can with energetic children and a dog the size of a horse.

On Tuesday, Roger came into the shop. As usual, he was all business. It seemed that whatever progress we had made in our relationship—which was almost nil—had evaporated away, and we were total strangers again. Had he noticed the busybodies talking at church? Had his mother harped on him again to avoid me?

I still hadn't given back Roger's manuscript. The story had captivated me and squeezed a tear from me at the appropriate moments. In fact, I'd bawled out loud, seeing Roger as the sailor and the story as a metaphor for whatever pain he silently carried in his heart.

Late that afternoon before Roger and Emily arrived home, I slipped the manuscript, with my notes as he'd requested, into a large manila envelope and put it on his doorstep. As I prepared to go to the Relief Society meeting at the ward building, he pulled into his parking space. I heard Emily's chatter and peeked through the curtains to see Roger turn the key, pick up the manuscript, and then walk in and close the door.

There. I had returned it. What a relief. He didn't have to speak to me again unless he wanted to. I had held on too long to the relationship that I thought would go somewhere, but yet it hadn't. I needed to move on with life.

I went dutifully to Relief Society. Did I want to be there? No, not really, but I could hear Aunt Lucy's voice telling me that I should "support Church activities because those in charge go to a lot of work to make it a wonderful experience for everyone." In the mood I was in, I would have preferred to stay home with Flo and fold laundry.

There were three service projects to choose from: quilting, assembling hygiene kits, or coloring pages for alphabet books. Halfway through the evening, I sat contently with a few other women, pushing huge, threaded needles through the multicolored squares that made up a quilt.

"I have noticed you sitting with Brother Wentworth in sacrament meeting," Sister Lilly remarked. "You seem to know him well. What is his story?"

"I actually don't know him well at all. Does he have a story?" I asked.

A sister named Karen joined in. "I heard he has a wife who had to be put away in an insane asylum. In one of her rages, she attacked Roger with a knife" —she lowered her voice to almost a whisper— "which accounts for the scar under his left ear."

Sister Lilly clicked her tongue in pity. "And he is such a good-looking man."

Roger is married? My head spun and I couldn't breathe, but I managed to say, "His wife may have been in a mental hospital, but she is in a private home now." The words "He's married!" ran through my head over and over again.

A younger sister joined in the conversation. "He has their little girl. Just think what that child has been through—a crazy mother, and having to be raised by a workaholic father. I'm surprised they live in our ward."

"What do you mean?" I said.

"Isn't he a big attorney for TriCorp Airlines? Surely he can afford to live in a better neighborhood than ours."

Roger had told me he was an attorney and he worked in downtown Tempe, but he hadn't mentioned that he worked for TriCorp. "Roger isn't a workaholic father," I countered. "He is a very attentive to Emily."

"I've seen you sitting with them at church, Janie, and walking home with the little girl," Sister Lilly declared. "In fact, a woman I talked to at the trunk or treat said you were living with him."

The quick bite of meatloaf I had for dinner now felt like a huge lump in my stomach. "It isn't true and you know it." I tried not to snap at her.

"Then how did she get that impression?"

"Well, we both live at Taylor Palms, and once when Roger wasn't home, he asked me to pack some clothes for his daughter. The woman you mentioned came looking for Roger while I was there." I resented having to explain anything to this gossip.

"Well," Sister Lilly said, not sounding completely convinced. "I only say this because I care about you. You'd better be careful getting too friendly with a married man. He *is* still married, you know."

No, I didn't know. I'd hoped he wasn't. Blood rushed to my face and I feared I looked as red as a tomato. Every sister in the circle stared at me and waited for my reply. I didn't want to reply. I wanted to leave the cultural hall and run home. My anger boiled.

"We are neighbors," I said, trying to control myself. "I've only taken care of Emily a few times when Roger needed me." I couldn't help standing, ready to put down the needle and walk out if necessary. "There is nothing between Roger and me—nothing at all!"

Sister Lilly stood too. Every needle in the circle was still. "My dear, I didn't mean to offend you. A pretty girl like you must make even married men's heads turn. I didn't mean anything by it."

Flattery must have been the right tactic. I took a deep breath, sat again, picked up my needle, and started tying, all the time wondering if these ladies would go home and tell their husbands about Sister Lilly's pretty-girl comment. I kept to myself for the rest of the meeting. It would only give the ward more to talk about if I'd walked out right then. I could have easily burst into tears, but somehow I managed to appear calm until the closing prayer. With the "amen" as my cue, and not waiting for the scrumptious-looking chocolate cake to be served, I slipped through the kitchen and out the door.

EIGHTEEN

If all the world hated you, and believed you wicked, while your own conscience approved you, and absolved you from guilt, you would not be without friends. . . .

God waits only the separation of spirit from flesh to crown us with a full reward. Why, then, should we ever sink overwhelmed with distress, when life is so soon over, and death is so certain an entrance to happiness—to glory?

Away from the scrutiny of my fellow sisters in the gospel, I let the tears fall. How could I have been so stupid? I'd only seen what I wanted to see. Now it was all so clear to me that he was married. Winnie was his love even if he didn't live with her. Poor Winnie! The women at Relief Society had called her crazy.

At home, I lay down on my bed and tried to relax the tension that tied my nerves in knots. Flo bounced over the bed and furniture to stand whimpering at the front door. I decided there was no rest for the weary, so I opened the door and followed Flo as she went outside. With a sigh, I turned the lawn chair around so I could see the temple while I let Flo run.

I looked up at the beautiful, serene sight that had always brought me peace. Relaxing into the chair, I breathed in the crisp late-fall air. What difference did it make what those women thought and said? I knew the truth—that was what mattered—and I'm sure my bishop would believe me if he heard any vicious rumors.

Roger's door stood ajar. It was nearly 9:00 PM and with Emily's bedroom dark, I assumed she was asleep. I leaned back and became lost in my thoughts while gazing at the few stars visible in the city limits.

Now I knew without a doubt that some of the sisters had gossiped about Roger and me behind my back. As soon as they realized I'd left the building, they had probably dissected my reaction to tonight's discussion. I couldn't remember a time when anyone really cared to talk about *any* man connected to me, but there was rarely a man in my life anyway.

After several minutes in deep thought, I decided I couldn't blame those poor, gossip-starved women. Most of our ward members were newlyweds or nearly, well, *finished*. Births and deaths were about the most exciting events that ever happened. And Roger is a very handsome man, so who wouldn't worry that I'd fall in love with him? I should've felt cared about, since these sisters hardly knew me yet still cared enough to warn me.

None of this logic consoled me in the least, and I began to cry quietly. The truth? I loved the man, married or not. Heavenly Father would have to forgive my unworthiness. I had slipped into this one-sided affair unknowingly and without any encouragement. I had never acted on my feelings or been dumb enough to declare them to Roger. Still, how could I be so dumb? Dumb! Dumb!

He wore no visible ring and had no visible wife, but he'd had a wife all along and I wouldn't let myself believe it. I didn't *want* to believe it. I had fantasized that someday he would fall in love with me and that he, Emily, Flo, and I would be a happy family, sealed in that beautiful building for all eternity.

(Well, the dog would have to wait outside.)

No wonder Roger kept his distance. No wonder he declined my invitations. How stupid of me not to see it! The best thing to do was to buy a house immediately and move away from the whole situation. I'd start looking for a place on Saturday morning.

"Flo, Emily has gone to bed." It was Roger's voice.

I turned to see Flo come out of the apartment with Roger following behind. I hurried to dry my face, thankful it was dark outside.

Still dressed in his work clothes minus the suit coat, Roger crossed the lawn. "Flo came looking for Emily, but she's asleep."

The dog came to me and put her head in my lap.

I tried to tell myself this man wasn't the most handsome I'd ever seen, but in the glow of the temple, he looked beautiful.

"I'm sorry she assumed she was welcome," I said. "She feels so at home at your place."

Roger tested the dryness of the grass before he sat. "That's all right. Emily considers Flo part of the family now."

"We think of Emily as family too."

We sat in the quiet for a moment. Passing cars created moving patterns of light on the trees. The silence felt awkward.

Finally, he spoke. "Janie, I was hoping I'd catch you tonight when you got home. We need to talk."

"That would be nice." Had he heard already about what happened at Relief Society?

"I—uh—I need to tell you that I'm married, if you haven't figured it out. Not that I think there is something between you and me, but just so I know that you know. I appreciate so much that you have taken Emily into your heart, and that she and Flo are such good friends. You've filled a void in her life. In mine too, you know? I just don't want us to get any closer than we are. We can't. Do you understand?"

I nodded, surprised but flattered by his frankness. My emotions were still close to the surface and I stroked Flo's head even harder. She loved the attention. I felt her slobber seep through my jeans.

Roger continued, "You've made this transition from her mother a little bit easier for her."

"From Winnie?"

He glanced up and then smiled. "I forget you are two people—the woman in the chocolate shop, and my neighbor who loves my daughter."

Sometimes I did feel like two people. "So why don't you wear a wedding ring?"

He looked at me with a cockeyed smile. "My wife, Winnie, is not well. She told me before we were married that she was bipolar. I had no idea what that meant. I tried to understand" —he shook his head— "but not until you live with it can you understand. And not unless it is inside of you can you *really* understand."

I nodded, trying to appear as if I knew what he meant.

"I married Winnie after a short courtship. Our parents pushed it. We were both from affluent families, and our parents were long-time acquaintances. I went along with it. And along the way I fell in love. I thought my love was authentic, but then I had always been obedient to my parent's wishes and I honestly tried hard to please them.

"Winnie's parents gave us the house on Val Vista Road as a wedding present. Winnie and I were happy that first year, until her condition worsened.

"The doctors changed her medications pretty often. They treated her for other things, too—depression, anxiety—but nothing ever made her well. Each drug worked for a little while, but before long she seemed to be back at the beginning again. In fact, she got worse as time went on. Her doctors now suspect she has something even more challenging than bipolar disorder. I don't understand any of it enough to explain it well."

Roger fell quiet again and rubbed his temples as I had seen him do many times under stress. After a moment he continued, "She would get violent or depressed and lock herself in her room for days. It would get ugly—her fits—and I'm ashamed to admit it now, but sometimes I'd yell back in frustration.

"One day we had gone out on the lawn—Winnie loved spending time outdoors, and nature seemed to calm her. With no explanation, she asked me for my ring. I slid it off and handed it to her. She studied it with an odd look in her eyes, then immediately turned and threw it into the trees. I couldn't believe it! I've searched several times for the ring, but with no luck. From that moment on, our relationship changed from one of working together to solve her problems, to her using her condition against me."

Poor Roger! Poor Winnie! I felt sorry for all they had to deal with.

"Yes, I should have bought another ring to wear, but I haven't had the heart to do it. But I still consider myself married—ring or not."

He sat for a moment with his elbows on his knees and his face in his hands. I didn't press him to continue, but he looked up, the worry evident in his eyes. "And now that you know the mess I'm in, you pity me, don't you?"

"No, I don't. Actually, I admire you for your strength. You have gone through so much alone."

"We aren't totally alone," Roger said with a sigh. "I tried having a nanny in our home, but it was too hard with Winnie around. My mother took care of Emily during the hardest times, and if it weren't for her, I don't know what I would have done. She still helps me out when she can. Mother has high hopes of Winnie getting well. Other people, friends and even some family members, have told me to get a divorce and move on with life. But Janie" —he looked at me intensely — "I believe in honoring my temple covenants. I can't live with her, but how can I throw her away only because she is hopelessly sick? I have to have faith she'll get well, faith like Mother has. I have to have hope in the covenants I've made in the temple and be true to the Lord and to Winnie."

I felt Roger's pain and wished I could put my arms around him and comfort him. I followed his gaze to that sacred monument before us. Another element I hadn't considered was that he was sealed for eternity to another woman and I'd never have claim. A treasure never mine, now slipped through my fingers. I took a deep breath to push away the heavy pain weighing on my heart.

"Emily needs so much care, and I can't give it to her and work too," he continued. "Winnie can't do it either. Luckily I found Becky, a woman who takes children into her home. I trust her. But the result is that Emily hardly knows her mother. I know Winnie loves Emily, but all Winnie can do right now is simply survive."

"That's why Emily loves Flo so much, isn't it?" It came to me almost like revelation. "Flo is pure love and giving."

"You're right." Roger stood and brushed the grass from his slacks. "All I can give you is my gratitude, Janie. Thank you for always being here to help me and for loving my daughter."

I stood and our eyes met for a moment. His were filled with pain, and I felt some of that pain. He extended his hand and I took it.

"Good night," he said quietly, then turned and went into his apartment and closed the door.

I sank into the lawn chair. Flo put her head in my lap again. I still felt warmed from Roger's touch and I wanted to cry more for the loss of it, but I had no tears left.

I rubbed my dog's head. "Florentine, at least I have you. You are a good dog, a good friend. Thank you for being so loyal." It was true, I knew, and one can't lie to a dog anyway.

In the relative quiet of the evening, best friends sat together for a few more minutes.

Life is crazy. You never know what it will serve you.

NINETEEN

"And how do people perform that ceremony of parting, Jane? Teach me; I'm not quite up to it."

"They say, Farewell.... Farewell Mr. Rochester."

"What must I say?"

"The same, if you like, sir."

"Farewell, Miss Eyre for the present; is that all?"

"Yes?"

My broken heart ailed me for the next week. My feet dragged. My smile was no longer spontaneous. Roger made no effort to let Emily spend time with Flo and me. They came home later every night. The light in Emily's bedroom would go out long past 8:00 PM. I could tell that Flo missed her terribly. I missed Emily too, and I tried to tell myself it was only Emily I missed. How could I miss a married man?

But I did. In my heart I knew the truth, so I confessed it right out loud. Now that I had recognized I had the problem, I could work on getting him out of my heart and mind.

Saturday came and Kylee and I spent the morning looking at houses, but I didn't find one I could see myself living in. There were so many beautiful houses with large, fenced-in yards and in nice neighborhoods. The only thing they lacked was a temple across the street.

At least I had my chocolate business to keep me busy. Our creative minds turned to autumn and Thanksgiving: cornucopias, harvest pumpkins, and wheat stalks; pilgrims and Indians. Jim Arnold promised a chocolate turkey to anyone in his weight-training classes who passed every physical feat on the requirement checklist, so we prepared ahead and made way more than enough.

Roger came into the shop the next Tuesday morning as usual to order the rose for Winnie. He obviously felt awkward.

"How's Winnie doing?" I asked, trying my best to sound cheery.

When he looked up, I saw the sadness in his eyes. "She's been doing better the last few days."

He looked above my head to study the pricing board. I waited. He never took this much time to order.

"Roger," I said in a businesslike tone, "if you'd like, we could set up an automatic account so that a rose will be delivered to Winnie every week. I could even choose something for Emily and bring it to her. Then you wouldn't have to come into the shop at all."

He looked down from the display and smiled. A knowing glint flickered briefly in his eyes, and I regretted suggesting the obvious solution to our dilemma. "Or I could give you the names of a few other chocolate shops in the area. None of them carry roses, though."

He nodded, biting his lip. "It has to be a rose."

"Would you like to set up the account, then?"

Roger paused. "All right," he finally answered. "What do I need to do?"

I pulled out a form and placed it and a pen on the counter in front of him. "All you have to do is fill this out and sign it to give us permission to charge the chocolate and the delivery fee to your debit card each week."

"The rose has to be delivered on Tuesdays."

"All right. I'll remember. Tuesday must be a special day for you." *It has been for me!* I wanted to say.

Roger signed the paper. "I proposed to Winnie on a Tuesday with a chocolate rose. We were both living in Provo then, going to BYU."

"There's no better way to say I love you, than with chocolate." I sounded like a commercial.

I watched him fill out the form as if I had talked a secret flame into signing my yearbook at graduation, knowing I would probably never see him again. *I've loved you all year,* I would have written in his book next to the picture of me with a terrible case of acne and a braces-intact smile.

So, I said goodbye again to Roger. To him, I was two people: the chocolate-shop clerk and his neighbor who loved his daughter, so two farewells seemed appropriate.

He put down the pen and handed me the form. "You know the address, but I put it on there anyway."

"Yes, thank you. We will take care of it. Let us know if anything changes." I slipped the form into a file for such orders that I'd later enter into the computer.

"All right. Goodbye, neighbor," he said. He hesitated as if he wanted to say more, and then he turned and hurried out of the store. I watched as the door closed behind him and then I stood there feeling empty and depressed and. . . .

I was sulking! A hallowed Tuesday-morning ritual had ended, just like that, and it was my doing. He would never step into my shop again. But I knew it had to be this way. I let out a long sigh and took a box from the stack to begin packing up one single chocolate rose for a woman that a wonderful man loved very much.

In the following days, I slipped deeper into sadness. The emotion was no stranger to me because I had worked through the grieving process after my parents and brother died in that horrible accident. Though my feelings upon losing a man I'd actually never dated, didn't compare to losing my parents, I now relived those days and feelings, too.

Eventually, I could hardly function at work. Even acting cheerful when waiting on customers was a burden. At home, I watched too much television, didn't want to go for walks, and slept whenever possible. After a time, even sleep became impossible.

Knowing I wasn't well, I arranged to take a few days off work and called Aunt Lucy to ask if I could come visit for a few days in Wickenburg. She didn't answer the phone or return my calls, so I emailed her. Her email reply read, "Dear Janie, I am in Ecuador building houses with Habitat for Humanity, but you are welcome to use my house for a few days. Sorry I won't be there to enjoy your visit."

I wasn't surprised. It was just like Aunt Lucy to be out saving the world.

Kylee took over full management of the shop and everyone else agreed to work more hours for a few days. Flo and I went to Wickenburg alone. We mourned. We slept. I ate a lot of chocolate. Besides chocolate always adding to my hips, it is all-around wonderful—and it's always available and cheaper than a therapist.

When our mourning days were over, we returned home, not feeling much better, but ready to start a new life without Roger and Emily Wentworth.

TWENTY

Gentle reader, may you never feel what I then felt? May your eyes never shed such stormy, scalding, heart-wrung tears as poured from mine. May you never appeal to Heaven in prayers so hopeless and so agonized as in that hour left my lips; for never may you, like me, dread to be the instrument of evil to what you wholly love.

I served on the Activities Committee in my ward. I forgot to tell you that because I'd forget it was my calling until Jill Ball called a planning meeting for the next event. Well, I received the phone call and dutifully attended.

We met on Thursday night in the Relief Society room. The church was empty otherwise, except for the bishopric meeting going on at the other side of the building. Four people attended the Activities Committee meeting: an older brother named Bernie who had a large mustache in need of trimming, a quiet woman named Mavis, and Jill and myself.

Jill wanted two Christmas parties for the ward. The family party would be a Saturday morning breakfast with Santa Claus. Jill had already thought it through, and she gave out the assignments. Bernie would be Santa, Mavis was in charge of the sing-along, and I was to flip pancakes and get the Santa costume cleaned. Jill handed me a big box stuffed with red flannel.

The evening before the breakfast with Santa, we'd hold an adults-only dinner party at the church building. Jill already had an idea for that, too. "It will be a Christmas-in-Hawaii dinner. We haven't had a ward luau for years, and they're a lot of fun. Santa will wear a hula skirt." Imagining Bernie wearing a hula skirt with his bushy mustache, I had to hold back a giggle.

"What happened to the Primary putting on a Christmas pageant?" Bernie asked. "I always liked that."

"Do you want to direct it?" Jill asked him pointedly.

"Well—" Bernie turned and looked at me.

I turned and looked at Mavis. She only wagged her head. The three now looked at me.

No way did I want to direct a Christmas pageant! I had only been in one as a child, and it wasn't a great memory. I was stuck on the front row of the chorus. Trevin Worliss thought it his duty to hold donkey ears over my head throughout the program, and when the leaders showed the video during Primary, I was the joke of the whole pageant.

"How about a Jamaican party? I know a good steel band," I said to change the subject.

Nobody even heard my suggestion, and the conversation turned back to the luau. I decided to try again. "An employee of mine named Carmen is in a Hawaiian dance group. They are mostly middle aged and older, but they put on a great show."

Jill looked doubtful. "Do they charge?"

"I don't think so."

"Great!" Jill said. "I don't care if they are from the geriatic hospital as long as they dance for free."

So, Jill assigned me to ask Carmen if her group could come perform at our Hawaiian Christmas luau, and if they'd do it for free.

The meeting ended and Jill walked with me to the parking lot, now full with the overflow from the temple parking. "I hear a new brother, Roger Wentworth, moved in next door to you."

"He and his four-year-old daughter." That sounded better, didn't it? I didn't want people to think Roger and I were over there alone together, with Sister Carter often out of town and all.

Jill unlocked her car. "Is it true his wife is crazy and that he owns the mansion on Val Vista Road where she lives?"

I didn't know how to answer. "I—I suppose. I don't know him very well at all."

"Really? I've seen you sitting with him at church. You look like you know him quite well."

Quite well? I thought. *We only sit on the same pew, miles apart.*

Jill lowered her voice. "You two have caused a bit of speculation around here."

What could I say? Next to Sister Carter, Jill was probably the best friend I had in the ward, which wasn't saying much. Did I owe her an explanation? "My dog and his daughter Emily are best friends. That's about the extent of it." Was this the time to spill the beans and pour out my disappointed feelings about falling in love with a married man?

I didn't think so either.

Jill scrutinized me with obvious disbelief before she opened her car door. "Call me as soon as you know about the hula group, okay?"

I nodded and said goodbye. Jill got into her car and drove away.

Several temple patrons walked past me on their way to their cars as I hurried down the street and around the corner to my house. When I came into the courtyard, I heard voices and noticed someone standing on Roger's doorstep. Even by the dim porch light, I recognized the woman who kept looking for him. I stepped into the shadows and listened.

"I saw two men leaving the park," Roger stated firmly. "I won't change my story just because you want to protect your boyfriend."

"There was only Jack!" the woman declared adamantly. "The other person was me. Me, I tell you. No one else. Maybe I looked like a man that day."

"You can make that claim all you want, but I told the police what I saw. I'm not retracting my statement."

"Then you are a liar! You self-righteous, pompous liar! All lawyers are liars and you're no different. You'll hurt for it later—you'll see." The woman stormed toward the street, but turned back to leave one last threat. "You will regret your stubbornness someday, *Mr.* Wentworth!"

Hearing the woman's angry voice, my blood ran cold. I watched her walk around the corner and disappear. No one came from the shadows to join her.

I moved quietly to my cottage. Roger still stood at his door. Our eyes met, and he tried to smile. How I wished I could go to him, but knew I shouldn't. I only nodded, unlocked my door, and went inside.

The day before Thanksgiving, Kylee and I packed up 106 four-inch chocolate turkeys to take to the high school for an after-school party honoring all students who passed Jim Arnold's physical-feat checklist. Kylee had arranged for her children to go to a friend's house after school. She left before 2:30 PM to deliver the turkeys and help hostess the party.

As we neared the end of November, business picked up in the shop. I figured gift giving had begun. No party should be without chocolate, and Christmas screamed "chocolate" from every store. I love downtown Mill Avenue at Christmastime with the decorations, the star and wise men on "A" Mountain, and the crowded sidewalks and shops. Christmas music blared from everywhere. Happiness reigned—exactly what I needed to get my mind off a certain man whose initials were Roger Wentworth.

Every night after closing the shop, I'd go home to my quiet cottage. Emily's light glowed until about 8:00 PM and then went out. At least Roger was keeping more regular hours. Anyway, if it weren't for Flo, I think I would've gone crazy. On a regular basis, I poured my heart out to her about Roger, and since she couldn't tell anyone, she was the perfect confidante.

Even living in the glow of the temple didn't bring the same joy anymore. Every time I saw its gleaming, white walls, I was reminded I had no one to take me there. And the man I had wanted for so long . . .

I knew if I didn't find a house soon, I would freak out and have a nervous breakdown or something. Seriously.

The ward Christmas luau, set for the first weekend of December, had been well advertised in the ward bulletins, and we put out a flyer announcing the event, with my cell phone as the contact number.

One question I wasn't expecting: "What's a luau?" came from Emily while we waited for sacrament meeting to begin the last Sunday in November. She examined the palm-tree graphic on the flyer. Roger, who had only nodded to me in greeting when he sat down, seemed deep in thought and hadn't heard the question.

"A luau is a party where everyone dresses up in flowered shirts and eats a lot of pineapple."

The little girl seemed happy with the abbreviated explanation. Just then, Roger looked up, so I asked, "Roger, why don't you invite Winnie to come to the ward luau? It'll be a lot of fun. We have some great entertainment planned." I had talked with Carmen and her dance group was all set.

Roger looked doubtful. "I don't know if Winnie is ready for crowds. I don't take her to restaurants because the noise makes her nervous."

"You told me she was doing better. Look, I'll help you. We'll put her between us at the dinner table and keep a close eye on her. If she starts feeling uncomfortable or anxious, you can take her home."

"I don't know—"

A twinge of guilt rushed over me. How could I put Winnie at risk because of selfish motives? The truth was, I thought if the ward sisters saw Winnie and Roger together and in my presence, they would stop gossiping.

The next morning, the shop stayed non-stop busy until afternoon. A happy Linc came to pick up the deliveries. Clearly, Jackie's disposition was rubbing off on him. "I'd like to invite you to my baptism in two weeks," he declared with a big grin.

Kylee and I stared as his words sank in.

"I'm being baptized into the Mormon Church!"

"Seriously?" Kylee asked.

I don't know why I doubted his sincerity. "Are you sure you aren't doing this for Jackie?"

"No!" he said, putting his hand on his chest. "I'm doing it for me."

"Is she still going on a mission?" I asked.

"She is. And I'll make it halfway through law school while she's gone." He smiled. "I can't believe how awesome I feel. When we talk about the Church, it is like I'm lifted out of my seat. Prophets, Apostles, Atonement, scripture—I feel as if I'm on fire!"

I stood all amazed. Kylee gaped.

So there you go—Linc had decided to join the Church, right under our noses. If we had pushed him into it, he would have never budged. It had taken a bubbly fireball named Jackie to make it happen.

TWENTY-ONE

I live in calm, looking to the end.

Looking forward to Linc's baptism gave me the lift I needed to get through the next few days. Carmen and I had worked late Thursday night making and pouring chocolate so I could take Friday off to help decorate and get the food ready for the luau. Kylee planned to manage the shop all day until Tessa and Frank arrived.

Roger decided to bring Winnie to the luau. He caught me on my way home late Thursday to tell me and ask if I was still willing to stay near them and help if necessary. Of course I said yes.

Wanting to support my committee, I found a bright yellow muumuu at Deseret Industries. The dress featured huge red and orange flowers, which of course only emphasized my hips. Since parking is at a premium around the temple during the Christmas lights and program, those of us who could were encouraged to walk to the meetinghouse for the luau. Carrying the freshly cleaned Santa outfit, I headed out my door and hurried toward the temple, worried that hungry bees might see my dress and think I was a flower in full bloom. Then I remembered that most bees hibernate in the winter, even in Arizona, so I was probably safe.

I walked into the cultural hall of the meetinghouse, looking like a blimp. As guests arrived, Bernie, wearing a Santa hat and a hula skirt, handed out plastic leis. I chose an orange one to go with my muumuu. Jill had gone home to change and came back in jeans and a Hawaiian-print blouse. She looked amazing. I wanted to hide in the ladies room for the rest of the evening. The only consolation was that the older sisters wore muumuus and looked like blimps too, including Sister Lilly.

Roger walked in with Winnie holding to his arm. They looked strange to me, probably because it was the first time I'd seen them together. I kept reminding myself they were married, not just on a date. Jealousy tried to raise its ugly head in my heart, but I beheaded it.

Winnie looked beautiful. No wonder Roger had fallen in love with her. The serenity of her lovely smile made it hard to believe she could be anything but congenial. Even though she also wore a muumuu, she looked delicate—the slender version of my blimpiness. The variety of blue shades in the dress material complemented her ebony hair and fair skin.

I greeted them. Winnie nodded politely and I realized she had been carefully drugged for this event. I don't think she remembered me as her weekly chocolate deliverer, for no hint of recognition showed in her eyes. Roger chose a table close to the back door of the cultural hall, obviously so they could escape quickly if anything happened.

As I helped set out food on the serving table, I saw Sister

Lilly and her husband stop by the Wentworths' table to say hello. Winnie smiled warmly.

Jill came next to me and set a big bowl of mixed fruit on the serving table. "She looks perfectly sane to me," she whispered, nodding toward the Wentworths.

"Maybe she is." I didn't feel like kindling the gossip.

Brother Toone offered the blessing on the food, and then most of the guests lined up, including Roger and Winnie. He kept his arm around her waist and spoke with the couple in front of them in line. The husband kept glancing from Roger to me, and then to Winnie. When everyone had filled their plates, I slipped back to the multipurpose room by the kitchen where Carmen and her dance troupe had gathered, including Willa with her fire-eating torch—unlit, of course.

"We're all set," Carmen told me. Bjorn said hello when he saw me, smiling his big, toothy grin. I showed Carmen the food we had set aside for the dance troupe.

"We can't eat before we dance," Carmen said. "Maybe after."

"Thank you for giving up your evening to perform for us," I said to Cricket.

"I'm cool with it." She hiccupped. "Doing a show is always fun." Then she banged a few times on her drum. "Hey, Janie," she said before I walked back to the cultural hall. "Where is Roger? I want to get a look at his wife." *Hiccup.*

"He's sitting in the back by the door."

She and Willa followed me into the hall and stuck their heads around the corner to get a look at Winnie.

Hiccup. "She's gorgeous!" Cricket said as I walked away.

I found my own plate and filled it with food, then took it to Roger's table and sat beside Winnie. She answered my questions with "yes" or "no," but otherwise didn't speak. She had a dazed look in her eyes, a clear sign that she was heavily sedated. I ignored stares from people at other tables and kept eating, hoping this appearance—the three of us together— would put a stop to any gossip about Roger and me.

When I finished eating, we cleared the tables. A dozen members of Carmen's dance group had set up and now waited in their places to begin the program. Bjorn sat in an empty seat at a front table, and I noticed him winking at Carmen. She wrinkled her nose and winked back. I had to laugh out loud at the two redheads who weren't dating.

While the last few plates were cleared away, drums beat and hips began swaying. I went back to my seat as Jill came out wheeling a cart full of pineapple upside-down cake, minus the dollop of chocolate I had suggested, and while we ate dessert, we watched the hula dancers. Even Winnie seemed delighted when Willa came out with a lit torch and began eating fire. That girl stuffed the torch right down her throat.

After several numbers, the dancers came to our tables and encouraged each of us to get on our feet and learn the hula. I reluctantly stood when a man with white hair took my hand and tried to pull me out of my chair. He got me swaying my hips and I probably looked like a blimp in a windstorm. When Willa pulled Roger up to dance, I glanced toward our table. Winnie now sat alone, quietly watching the show. I peered over at Roger, who, like the rest of us, looked quite ridiculous doing the hula.

I tried to keep an eye on Winnie, but lost direct sight of her when my instructor pulled me through the crowd to the other side of the dance floor, saying we'd have more room there.

Soon, the song ended and I went back to our table to find it empty.

Roger returned too. "Where's Winnie?" he asked as we sat down.

"She was here a minute ago." We glanced around the cultural hall, Roger clearly nervous.

The final number began. As far as I could tell, everyone was seated with no empty chairs—except Winnie's. "Do you think she's in the ladies room?" I asked.

"She wouldn't have gone alone." Roger stood. "She wouldn't have gone anywhere alone."

He headed toward the foyer. I followed him and then headed to the restroom. I called Winnie's name, but it only echoed on the tiled walls.

Roger went outside and I waited. "No sign of her," he said as he came back in the building. "I wonder what got into her to wander off like this."

I searched the halls and nooks and classrooms. No sign of Winnie anywhere. Roger ran outside again and sprinted around the perimeter of the meetinghouse.

Hurrying back to the cultural hall, I was worried all the way down to my painted toenails. "Roger's wife is missing!" I told Bernie, who was master of ceremonies and was bringing the program to a close. He stopped midsentence to listen to my hysteria.

"She isn't well and can't be alone." At Bernie's urging, I stepped up to the microphone and announced, "Sister Wentworth has wondered off. We need help."

Roger came hurrying in. "No sign of her."

No one seemed to know what to do. Some volunteered to go out and search for her.

"Let's have a closing prayer," Bernie said. "Then those who can stay will search the building inside and out. Brother Jones, will you dismiss us?"

Brother Jones said a wonderfully short but pleading prayer. The men quickly organized and went outside in different

133

directions. Some went into the surrounding neighborhood; others went to search the crowds viewing the Christmas lights on the temple grounds. The sisters and I began another search of the classrooms. The first door opened to the nursery. Sister Lilly followed right behind me.

"Janie, there was something strange tonight. I think someone kidnapped Sister Wentworth and I witnessed it, but of course at the time I thought nothing of it."

I should've asked Sister Lilly first, since she usually knows everything that happens in the ward. "What did you see?" I asked.

"After the dancers came to our tables, I saw a man help Winnie out of her chair to get her to dance. I hadn't seen him in the show earlier, but his Hawaiian-print shirt fit in with everyone else's, so I didn't think anything of it. I only watched a few seconds because I started dancing too. But, Janie, that man probably took her right out the front door and no one even noticed!"

TWENTY-TWO

Here I walked about for a long time, feeling very strange, and mortally apprehensive of some one coming in and kidnapping me; for I believed in kidnappers, their exploits having frequently figured in Bessie's fireside chronicles.

With Sister Lilly still beside me, I called 911 and explained our dilemma. Then I called Roger's cell phone. "Any luck yet?"

"No," he answered. Poor Roger! I could hear the panic that gripped his heart. I told him Sister Lilly's theory, and that I had called 911.

No one wanted to leave. Even Willa, Carmen, Cricket, and most of the dancers stayed. After they searched a while, the dancers ate their dinner. The cleanup committee stayed long after they finished their work.

We moved as a group to the parking lot. I felt helpless and had a sick feeling in the pit of my stomach. Cricket stood beside me and fretted. Soon she began to pace across the blacktop, big tears wetting her cheeks. I'd never seen her in such a state.

Roger and many of those who had gone out searching returned, saying there was no sign of Winnie anywhere.

Sister Lilly approached Roger and said, "Now that I think about it, I'm certain the man who danced with Winnie wasn't in the dance group. His arms were covered with tattoos. I would have noticed something like that during the program if he'd been dancing."

Carmen leaned close to my ear. "None of the men in our dance group have tattoos."

"This is scary," I said to Roger.

His eyes held an increasingly fearful look, and he kept rubbing his forehead as I had seen him do so many times. "I should have stayed with her," he muttered helplessly.

"Don't blame yourself," I said. "Blame me. I said I would help if you needed me, and when the crucial moment came, I wasn't there."

"Janie, there's no way we could have expected something like this." He looked me in the eyes for the first time that evening. "I wish I hadn't got caught up in the show. I should have stayed with her."

My heart ached for him. I put my hand on his arm and he placed his over mine. "Pray hard, Janie," he said. "If we don't find her tonight, well, she'll go crazy without her meds. I'd hate to see what would happen."

Listening to our conversation, Cricket went pale. I put my arm around her and found her trembling.

"We'll find Winnie," I assured her. "Don't worry."

The police arrived and Roger told them the whole story. Then Sister Lily gave a description of the suspected kidnapper. "I thought, how sweet of him to get Sister Wentworth involved. You know—because of her—" she looked at Roger.

"She is mentally ill," he told the officer.

"Yes, we are aware of that. We have patrolmen on the streets right now. If she's on foot, she won't get very far."

We waited another hour. Still no sight of Winnie.

Some ward members drove or walked around the neighborhood, while others waited at the meetinghouse. Bjorn assisted in the search until Carmen called him back so they could take Cricket home. The girl now shook in her mother's arms, causing her grass skirt to quiver.

After many of the searchers returned to the parking lot, Roger decided to check his apartment, even though he never took Winnie there. A police officer accompanied him to the apartment, while I waited anxiously at the meetinghouse with several other ward members.

Roger still hadn't returned when the officer in charge decided everyone should go home. "None of you can do anymore tonight, so you might as well get some rest," he said. "We will keep searching and doing all we can to find Mrs. Wentworth."

After talking for a few minutes, the group reluctantly disbanded, and I walked the short block alone to my house. The streets felt deserted. With the Christmas lights at the temple turned off long before, the parking lots echoed emptiness. An eerie, cool breeze danced in the leaves still clinging to the branches. A lone figure stood in Taylor Palms' courtyard as a police car pulled away.

Roger only glanced at me when I came through the gate. "I don't know what to do next." He sighed in defeat. He hung his head for a moment, then looked up and clenched his fist. "I'm sure Malinda and her boyfriend took Winnie. It's another attempt to get me to change my story."

I'd had the same thought several times. "It seems a bit inhumane to take an ill woman."

"I've never made her condition public." Roger walked

over to where I stood on the lawn. "They could have as easily taken you."

"Me? Why?"

He looked down at me, frustration and fear evident in his eyes. "They think we are—that you mean something to me." He looked away. "It is logical."

Logical? Because you say hello to me once in a while? But then I remembered the times we had spoken together in the courtyard, that we had sat on the same pew in church, and that Malinda had found me in Roger's apartment.

"They don't know how ill Winnie truly is." Roger ran his hand through his hair.

"Well, then they will find out soon enough," I said too hastily. I hoped my bluntness hadn't offended Roger, but he went on without reacting.

"She can't go even an hour past her medication time. Who knows what she'll do?" He took a few more steps toward the street. "I don't even know where to look for her. We've searched the entire neighborhood. She has to be safe! I won't be able to live with myself if they harm her."

My mind conjured up all sorts of horrors.

"I should've never left her alone at the table," Roger mumbled, almost to himself. His eyes became glassy. "I should never have brought her."

"Don't say that, Roger. I'm the one who told you to bring her."

He turned, took hold of my shoulders, and looked me squarely in the eyes. "I don't want you carrying any guilt. This isn't your fault." He let go and ran his hand through his hair again. "I can't stop thinking the worst! Maybe the kidnappers won't want to deal with her illness so they'll take her out to the desert and leave her there, or maybe they'll even k—" Roger stopped midword, looking at me in horror.

Suddenly, I felt the cold, and it wasn't just the late-night air. "Don't even think that way, Roger! We will find Winnie before anything happens to her. Plus, they would be crazy to harm her, since they'd only get in more trouble."

He turned away and glanced at me over his shoulder. "They want to hurt me. They want me to change my story—to give up. They warned me that they'd retaliate if I didn't lie about what I saw. Now I must choose between honesty and saving my wife."

"Roger, what did you see?"

He walked away and I thought he might go into his apartment, but he motioned for me to sit with him on the lawn. I sat in my lawn chair and he sat on the grass beside me. "I guess it's time to tell you the whole story."

There's more? "You don't have to tell me if you don't want to."

Roger's look changed from worry to sorrow. "You are involved in this now, so you deserve to know the whole story." He picked up a twig and threw it. "It all happened well over a year ago. Winnie had been doing better on her medication, and life had become somewhat normal. We were living in the Val Vista house, and I had high hopes our troubles were over. This particular afternoon, we left Emily at my mother's and went up on the Salt River to Granite Reef so that Winnie could paint at the riverside. She is an excellent artist and has made somewhat of a name for herself."

"Really?" I almost laughed, thinking of the very sedate woman who had accompanied Roger that evening. I tried to fit what I knew into a life of fame.

"The water always seemed to calm her and give her hope. The ocean had the same effect, and we went to San Diego as often as we could."

I nodded. "You are a devoted husband."

He laughed hollowly. "I've tried." He looked out to the street as a car passed. "We had been at Granite Reef for a while and I was getting hungry, but Winnie didn't want to leave until she had enough of the painting that she felt she could finish at home. She told me to go back to the hamburger stand a few miles into town. They serve tacos—she has a thing for tacos." He smiled to himself. "I should've known better, but she kept assuring me she'd be fine. The park had been peaceful for hours, and she seemed so content at the easel. I realize now it was foolish to leave her, just like I left her tonight." Roger shook his head and rubbed his face.

"While I was gone, three men came into the park and had a fight. It was two against one and the lone man was killed. They left the body in the bushes and threw the knife in the undergrowth by the road. Winnie saw the whole thing, but they never saw her.

"When I got back, I saw the two men running up to the park entrance. One threw something into the bushes—probably the knife. I had passed their car parked on the highway and hadn't thought much about it except that it looked unsafe perched on the shoulder of the road. I also noticed the young woman standing by the car. She stared at me for several seconds, so I remember her face clearly."

"It was Malinda?"

Roger nodded. "I ran to where I'd left Winnie, but she was gone, and her easel and paint palette were on the ground. I looked everywhere and started to panic because the sun was beginning to set. In the shadows, I practically stumbled over the body. He was dead but still warm and cut up pretty badly—stabbed. Seeing him scared me good. I feared the murderers had thrown Winnie in the river. Finally, after frantically calling her name several times, I heard her crying. I found her far down the riverbank under a bush, scared into hysterics."

"Poor Winnie!"

"After that day, her mental health crashed. Witnessing a murder put her over the edge. I couldn't handle her on my own anymore, and after much counseling and thought, her doctor admitted her to a mental hospital."

"Eden's Garden," I put in.

"Yes," Roger replied. "Those people were so good to her. They helped her become somewhat stable—enough that I thought I could bring her home. I found a team of reputable caretakers who would stay with her around the clock. But the only one Winnie can even tolerate is Grace, so she has kindly taken on practically her full care, with very few hours of relief. I felt it was better for Emily if she and I moved elsewhere and only came to visit. That is why we moved here."

"So, you didn't actually witness the murder?"

"Only after the fact. Winnie saw the whole thing, but not being well, she didn't have to testify in court. I did, and that's why Malinda decided to stalk me. To this day she maintains that my story is wrong—that Jack did the deed alone, that it was only her, Jack, and the dead man who went for a drive that day, and that Jack and the man had a fight. Jack is in jail because his fingerprints matched one of the sets on the knife, and because I identified him. The authorities arrested him right away and Malinda made the mistake of showing up at his hearing. She got off light for being an innocent bystander—three months in jail for not coming forward to report the crime. But why Jack sides with her story, I don't know."

I sat stunned. "How traumatic for Winnie to have to deal with all this!"

"I wish I could reach into her mixed-up brain and pull out that memory, and pull out all the craziness in that beautiful head of hers, so she can be the woman I fell in love with."

Roger put his face in his hands and groaned in anguish before he looked up again. "The police believe my story because there is another set of fingerprints on the knife besides Jack's, and they aren't Malinda's or the victim's." Roger looked up. "Jack had a juvenile record for car theft, so they had his prints on file. The other man hasn't been identified."

"You could identify Malinda from seeing her only once?"

"Yes, I knew her immediately when I saw her again at the hearing. She saw me too. It was an awkward moment. We stared at each other in one of those 'I-know-you-don't-I?' moments. I could see the wheels turning in her head.

"Of course, she heard me testify about everything I saw, including seeing her. I tried to keep Winnie out of my testimony as much as possible, but the murderers have figured out she was there and knows something."

I couldn't imagine being in such a fix. "Murders like that only happen on television."

"You'd think," Roger said. "I wish we hadn't gone out there that day. I wish I hadn't left Winnie to go get the food. She relapsed and her recovery has taken so long. I wish I hadn't left her at the table tonight. No telling what tonight will do to her—or what the murderers will do to . . ."

"Wishing doesn't do anything." I swept my open hand across his back. "Pray. Pray that the police find her."

How could a person as ill as Winnie come through a kidnapping with no repercussions without divine help?

My cell phone vibrated in the pocket of my muumuu. The caller ID read, "Restricted." Hoping it was someone with news about Winnie, I answered, "Hello?"

TWENTY-THREE

It is far better to endure patiently a smart which nobody feels but yourself, than to commit a hasty action whose evil consequences will extend to all connected with you; and besides, the Bible bids us return good for evil.

T he caller spoke in a low, calm voice. "Is this Janie?"

"Yes. Who is calling?"

Another long pause. "My name doesn't matter," the man said. "Tell Mr. Wentworth I have his wife. Tell him he doesn't get her back until he changes his story about the murder."

"Who is this? How did you get my number?"

"You don't need to know who this is. Your number, Janie, was on the party invite." The man laughed. "Tell Roger to meet me at the school down the street from the church so we can discuss how to get his wife back, and he better not bring the police."

"I'll tell him but—but Winnie isn't well," I blurted. "She'll go crazy without her medications." I glanced to see Roger's reaction, but he only stared at me anxiously.

The caller paused. Roger held out his hand for the phone and I gladly surrendered it to him.

"Who is this?" he demanded. "Yes, this is Roger. Where? Leave her alone! She isn't well, she's . . . all right." He ended the call and handed the phone to me, the worry intensifying in his eyes. "The basketball court at Mesa Junior High."

"The school is down the street."

He grabbed my arm and started toward his car. "You're coming with me."

"I—I shouldn't."

"No?" Roger stopped and looked at me with pleading eyes.

I drew away from his stare. "You're married and we shouldn't be alone."

"To heck with all the gossips!" He grabbed my arm and started toward his car again. "My wife has been kidnapped and you have to help me!"

He pulled open the passenger door of the Prius and I got in. He ran around the front of the car and slid into the driver's seat. (I felt awkward, in case you were wondering.) He started the car and we were on 2nd Avenue and past the dark church building before I could gather my thoughts.

How many times had I dreamed of sitting next to Roger in his car—on a date, of course? I'd given up the dream when I'd learned he was married, and in our current circumstances, my feelings were quite the opposite of heavenly.

Roger parked across the street from the school basketball courts. "Stay in the car, Janie. Keep low and listen. If you hear a gunshot or anything out of the ordinary, or if I don't come back, call the police."

"Shouldn't I call the police anyway?"

"No. Let me see if Winnie is all right. If I don't find her

after fifteen minutes, then *I* will call the police."

Roger got out and closed the door soundlessly. I watched him disappear into the darkness along the chain-link fence that surrounded the basketball courts. I listened. There was only silence until a car rattled by. I slid down in the seat and waited. The smell of fried onions drifted on the cold breeze that caused the treetops to sway softly. Several minutes went by. A tall teenage boy dressed in dark, baggy shorts and a sweatshirt slid along on a skateboard. *Clink, clink, clink*, the wheels sang, hitting every crack in the sidewalk. The sound faded away as the boy disappeared down the street. A sliver of a moon appeared above the rooftops.

After saying about my hundredth quick prayer that night, I looked towards the basketball courts but saw no movement. My impatience got the best of me. Opening the door as quietly as possible, I got out of the car. Then I hurried across the street, ran along the fence, and ducked behind a humming electrical box nestled up against it. As I watched and waited, all I could hear was its soft hum and my own nervous, erratic breathing.

"Whatcha doing here?"

Startled, I looked up into the face of a stranger. I tried to scream, but the man slapped his hand firmly over my mouth. "Come on," he ordered, pulling me to my feet.

As terror filled my heart and my brain started to buzz, my limbs became useless. Since I could do little more than stand, my kidnapper practically dragged me toward the school. I prayed silently (I could do that), begging the Lord to save me—and to save Roger and Winnie.

I tried to look at the man, but all I could see of him were his tattooed arms.

He tightened his grip and I squirmed in pain. He didn't loosen up and when I regained some strength in my legs, I ran to keep pace with him. Once we were hidden from the street by a building, he tossed me onto the concrete, where I collided with another body. I recognized the beautiful, dark hair right away.

"Winnie! Are you all right?" I cried, scrambling to my knees—a difficult feat while wearing a muumuu.

The kidnapper had tied her hands in front of her with a thin rope. Winnie lifted her head and spat out, "Yes, I'm fine!"

She glared up at our abductor, and I saw the man fully for the first time. He had a balding head ringed by a fringe of brown hair, and a double chin. With muscular arms and broad shoulders, the man perfectly fit Sister Lily's description, right down to the bulging belly.

He pulled me to him again. "Who are you!" he shouted in my face.

I didn't answer. The tobacco on his breath made me gag. A mischievous smile spread across his face and he dropped me to the ground. *Ouch!*

"You're the girl who lives with Wentworth. Ha, ha! So, here we have Wentworth's gorgeous but loony wife and his pretty little girlfriend."

I took hold of Winnie's arm and tried to keep my voice calm so she wouldn't be alarmed. "Winnie, you know he is lying. Trust me, there is nothing between Roger and me."

I looked at the man. "Let us go!" I demanded as bravely as possible. "What will you gain by keeping us here?"

"Shut up!" He pulled a small revolver from his pocket and stuck it in my face.

I squeezed my eyes shut and prayed he wouldn't shoot. Twenty-seven years old is too young to die!

"Having both of you here ought to merit some leverage with that high-and-mighty Wentworth lawyer," he said, then straightened. "I've got a trump card and I'm gonna play it."

The man continued pointing the gun toward us as he walked backward to the corner of the building and hollered, "Hey, Wentworth!" His voice echoed against the dark, empty breezeway. "I've got your wife *and* your lover here. Had to bring her along, didn't you? Ca-sa-no-va! Are you ready to talk?"

I held my breath as seconds passed with no answer. Then Roger's voice echoed in the distance. "Sure. I'm ready."

"Then come over here." He stepped out in plain view and looked toward the sound of Roger's voice.

After several seconds, Roger called, "Meet me on the basketball court. Bring the girls with you."

The tattooed man glanced toward us and chuckled, making his belly shake. He shouted angrily, "The girls stay. You come here." The stranger held up the gun again, checked it, and then slid it into his pocket.

"Roger!" I screamed, desperate to warn Roger about the gun, but the man pulled it out and aimed it toward me before I could say more.

"SHUT UP!" he sneered, pausing between the words for emphasis.

I shut up. I could feel Winnie trembling beside me, so I put my hand on her arm in an attempt to calm her. "Pray, Winnie," I whispered.

"Stay here and don't move, or your man is dead!" the kidnapper snarled.

For several more seconds, he kept the gun pointed toward me. I couldn't see Roger from where I sat on the gritty sidewalk, but the sound of his footsteps echoed off the brick and concrete walls.

I remembered the cell phone in my pocket but didn't dare take it out with the gun pointed toward me, so I waited. As soon as the man took a step around the corner, I would pull out my phone and call the police.

Just then, the sound of sirens pierced the night. The footsteps stopped. The sirens screamed, coming closer every second. I hoped and prayed they were coming for us. More sirens wailed from the east. A river of obscenities streamed from the stranger before he yelled, "Wentworth!"

And then a gunshot.

Winnie put both hands to her head and started screaming. It sounded exactly how you'd think a woman at her wits' end would scream—high and shrill. I kept my grip on her, but her screeching continued and bounced off the walls and concrete surrounding us.

The man swore again and rushed back to us. He grabbed Winnie's shoulders and shook her violently. "Stop it! Stop screaming!"

But she wasn't as obedient as I had been.

He gave up and thrust the gun in his pocket. Then, leaving Winnie, he grabbed my wrist and pulled me up and with him into a run. I heard Winnie scream, "Janie!" and then fall into hysterics.

The man was too heavy to move quickly, and he panted as we ran down the long breezeways of the school. Winnie must have quit screaming, because I could hear only my own heart pounding and the man's huffing. I had to think of something, but what?

Then, conveniently, I tripped on the uneven sidewalk and tumbled onto the grass, pulling the man down on top of me. He cursed while scrambling to his feet. "Get up!" he ordered with a yank on my wrist.

"My ankle!" I feigned, grabbing it in pain. "I twisted my ankle." *Ouch!* The real pain throbbed in my hip, and for the first time I was thankful for extra padding.

He yanked on my arm again, but I gritted my teeth and played the part of dead weight. "Get up!" he growled furiously.

"I can't! It's hurts too bad!" I cried. "I think it's broken."

The sirens drew nearer and he panicked. "Get up! You're faking!"

He kicked me as if I was a stubborn mule. I started wailing as obnoxiously as I could; I even produced real tears. The man looked around in obvious fright, then ran down the corridor and toward the parking lot. I heard a door slam and a motor start and rumble away. The whole scene probably took less than three minutes.

The sirens ceased their wailing. I stood gingerly and rubbed at the smart from the fall and the kick, then retraced my path. Winnie sat quivering in a pathetic huddle in the same spot on the sidewalk.

I pulled her to her feet and put my arms around her. "He's gone," I assured her. "Let's find Roger." Fortunately, the abductor was no Boy Scout, and I easily removed the ropes from Winnie's wrists. (Flo could've untied those knots!) After freeing Winnie, I held to her and we hurried through the dark to find Roger.

A lone figure came from the shadows toward us. "Roger!" I screamed. "Roger!"

"Winnie!" Roger ran into the light and caught her in his arms. She trembled as he held her close and spoke softly.

Breathing hard, I stepped back and wrapped my arms around myself, hardly believing I was alive. An overwhelming feeling of relief swept over me as I said a silent prayer of thanks.

I felt a pang of jealousy as I watched Roger hold Winnie. Naturally, he would want to comfort her. She had all rights to him.

Before the police reached us, Roger turned to me. "Are you all right?"

Even though I felt jittery inside and feared my knees would give way, I nodded.

"We got your call," Officer Ward said to Roger as he approached us. "Is anyone hurt?"

Policemen piled from their cars and began searching the campus.

"I think we're all fine," Roger answered breathlessly. "Please don't call an ambulance. I don't think Winnie could handle being treated by paramedics, or going to the hospital.

"But he shot the gun!" I interjected. "Are you okay?" I tried not to sound too emotional.

"I'm fine. I don't think the guy ever saw me."

"I'm glad you found Mrs. Wentworth," Officer Ward said. Then he began asking Roger and me questions. Winnie hid her face against Roger's shoulder, refusing to even look at the officer.

Finally, Roger said, "I need to get my wife home." He started to move her toward his car on the street. "She isn't well enough to give any information."

Winnie raised her head and struggled to speak. "It—it was the murderer," she finally uttered.

"The murderer at the river?" Roger took her by the shoulders and looked into her face. "Are you sure?"

Winnie nodded and ran her trembling hand along her other arm.

"His arms are tattooed," I interpreted. Winnie laid her head against Roger's chest.

He looked helplessly at the officer, and the man nodded. "Take her home, Roger. I'll meet you at your house."

As Roger and Winnie started toward his car, Officer Ward

turned to me. "Janie, will you show me where the abductor held you and Mrs. Wentworth?"

"Sure." I led him and another officer down the sidewalk and around the corner. There was no evidence of two women huddling there only minutes before, terrified for their lives. Next, with the two officers following me, I retraced the path from where the kidnapper had dragged me through campus to where I fell, and then to the parking lot. I showed them the spot where I figured the man's vehicle, which I never saw, had been parked.

To my surprise, Roger waited for me to return. Winnie already sat in the car. He opened the back door as I walked toward him. Officer Ward said goodbye and went to his patrol car.

"I can walk home," I told Roger. Surely, he didn't want a tag-along at this crucial, tender moment.

"I can't let you walk when those criminals could still be around." He kept the door open, waiting expectantly.

That made sense. I certainly didn't want to be the murderer's target practice, and my pride could handle a few more uncomfortable minutes, so I climbed into the back seat. I began to suspect that the stress of the evening had affected Roger's sense of direction, because he drove east from the school. I watched longingly over my shoulder as we drove out of the familiar neighborhood.

Winnie sat with eyes downcast. No one said a word, and I tried to concentrate on the soft whir of the engine. Roger reached over and took Winnie's hand. She lifted her chin but only stared ahead, tears rolling freely down her face. After a long silence, he said to her, "Do you want to talk?"

She freed her hand from his and hid her face with it. That's when I wished I were a fly so I could crawl through the tiny open slit in the window and fly home.

Grasping the steering wheel with his left hand, Roger ran his right hand over Winnie's shoulder. "Are you all right? Did they hurt you?"

Her dark curls fell over her shoulders as she shook her head no. Then she leaned forward slightly and Roger rubbed her back. Suddenly, she started to giggle, softly at first, then louder and louder. When she threw back her head and wailed in hysterics, I wished again to be that fly.

Roger gripped the steering wheel with both hands. As if he knew my thoughts, he spoke softly to me over his shoulder, "Be patient."

Winnie's wails turned into high-pitched laughter, then tear-producing sobs. Finally, she dropped her face into her hands and wept quietly.

Roger gently rubbed her shoulder again. "I'll get you home soon. We can talk about it there."

TWENTY-FOUR

"I knew," he continued, "you would do me good in some way, at some time: I saw it in your eyes when I first beheld you; their expression and smile did not strike delight to my inmost heart so for nothing."

We cruised down Main Street through every light on green. Roger pulled his cell phone from his pocket and dialed. "We found Winnie. She's shook up, but we're on our way home." There was a long pause. "Yes, everyone is safe." Another pause, then, "Please get her room ready. Thanks." He slid his phone closed.

The dashboard clock showed it was long after midnight. Roger turned the car onto Val Vista. Once again, I felt like an intruder. Why had he dragged me along, anyway? He could've just as easily dropped me off at my apartment, or I could've taken my chances and walked home. I would've simply ducked behind one of those black rubber garbage cans every time a car passed. Then again, I doubt that even an oversized garbage can could hide my bright yellow muumuu. Besides, trash pick-up in that area—my neighborhood—was on Thursday, so most people had already taken their cans off the street.

I felt safer in the back seat. And although I couldn't wait to get home, I feared that wouldn't happen anytime soon. At the Val Vista house, several police officers waited in their cars on the street. Roger punched numbers into the security gate box, and when the gate opened, the police cars followed us into the estate. As Roger pulled the car up the softly lit driveway, the front door of the house opened and a woman wearing nurse's scrubs stepped out and hurried to the passenger door. She opened it and helped Winnie out and walked her to the porch. Roger got out as well. "Are you coming in?" he asked me through the window.

"I think I'll wait here."

"Well, there's a law book on the floor back there. It makes great reading." He tossed me one of his gorgeous lopsided smiles.

I glanced down to see the five-inch-thick volume near my feet. "I'm sure I'll enjoy it."

"If you get too bored, come on in."

After I nodded in agreement, Roger joined the police officers gathering around the front door.

One officer came to the car window as the others went into the house with Officer Ward. "I'd like to get a full statement from you while you're not with the others. Do you mind?"

I got out of the car and gave my story again as the officer sat on a stone bench by the porch and typed on his laptop. I tried to remember every detail, right down to the details of the man's tattoos.

"Please come to the station tomorrow," the officer said, "and we'll do a composite sketch of the kidnapper. What time will you be available?"

"By 10:00, I guess." Breakfast with Santa started at 8:00.

The officer went into the house, and I didn't know what else to do, so I got back in the back seat of Roger's car to wait. No way did I want go inside and be in the way. I picked up the law book and thumbed through its pages. The book had hardly any pictures and a lot of small print, which I couldn't make out in the dim light.

I vowed to compliment Roger on his taste in entertaining literature.

Time dragged on, and finally I lay down on the seat. I dozed off and on, vaguely recognizing the sound of an occasional car passing on the street, a nocturnal bird squawking, or a horn in the distance. Wearing only the thin dress, I felt chilly. I found a sports duffel stashed under the seat, so I pulled out a hand towel and covered my shoulders. Then, using the bag and the rest of its contents as a pillow, I lay in the dark and wished again that I had walked home.

But something else bothered me too. Something deeper. I tried to draw it out so I could dissect it and understand. A vision of Winnie in Roger's arms kept coming to my mind. *Is that it—jealousy?* Logically, I knew she belonged in his arms, so that wasn't it.

I searched my heart and the vision became clearer, and as it did, I began to sob, only sniffles at first, but then a waterfall. I had experienced major trauma—the terror of a gun in my back, a gun in my face, and knowing that Roger or Winnie could be harmed as well.

Winnie had Roger to be strong for her, to be there for her. But I had no one to be strong for me, or to hold me after the danger passed. I had no one to run to, no one who even cared besides Kylee and Florentine. A sister and a canine aren't a replacement for a man who loves you.

I was alone in the world and I knew it too well. I always told myself that since I had Kylee as a sister and best friend, and as long as I had a bishop to rely on if needed, I'd be fine. I'm a strong woman, and if I never had a chance to marry, at least in this life, I could handle it. But at that moment, after watching Roger comfort and take care of Winnie, reality stared me right in the face, and it wasn't pretty.

My sobs became uncontrollable and the more I cried, the better I felt, as if emptying buckets of sorrow from my burdened heart. I had to go on alone, for there was no one to go on with—except the Lord. And that would be all right, because I knew He loved me. My soul began to calm. Yes, He loves me, and at that moment I knew He was aware of my sorrow.

I don't remember falling asleep again, but the car was moving when I awoke. I sat up and looked at Roger in the driver's seat, then at the clock on the dashboard. It read 2:00 AM.

Roger glanced at me in the rearview mirror. "Hello. Get any rest?"

"Yeah," I said groggily, smoothing down my bed-head. "Is Winnie all right?"

"She is now. We gave her meds and put her to bed. She was resting when I left. You slept through all the excitement."

"No, I think I saw the best of it." I vividly recalled the sight of a loaded revolver pointed at me and Winnie, and I attempted to think about something else. Like the fact that Roger could've been killed too. *No, wait, that won't work either.* With a sigh, I relaxed into the seat and counted streetlights in passing. One, two, three. My eyes drooped. "I didn't realize how tired I am."

"This has been quite a night," Roger said wearily. The temple came into view, still lit up, as always, even at this late hour. We were nearing home. "After I left you in the car at the school, I never saw anyone, so I called the police. Right after that, the kidnapper called out to me. Good timing, huh?"

"Couldn't have been better."

"I never saw the man," he said, glancing again at me in the review mirror. "You told the officer the guy was covered in tattoos, so I'm sure it is the same thug I saw at the park. He is the one Malinda's been protecting."

He got out of the car, opened my door, and offered his hand to help me out. I smoothed my rumpled muumuu and resolved to never wear it again. At my next luau, I'm wearing tight jeans and a hibiscus-print blouse. We walked into the courtyard. Home felt good.

As I stopped and looked up at Roger, my emotions suddenly threatened again. "Tomorrow I'm going to the police station to help make a sketch of the kidnapper."

"Good." He hesitated. "Thank you, Janie, for helping me tonight, even though I put you at risk and you almost got killed. And especially for going out to the house with us. Having you along gave me support. Sometimes I feel so alone in this battle, this never-ending nightmare. I'm sorry you lost a good night's rest."

I swallowed and tried to blink away tears. "It was a spectacular ending to a great luau. I'll never forget it." Obviously, quick wit was beyond my capacity at that moment. "I'm glad we found Winnie and that she's okay."

He nodded. I reached out my hand and he took it. "Good night," he said but still didn't leave. He looked at me, but I couldn't meet his eyes. "You've been crying."

I looked away. My emotions were too close and the tears started.

"Tell me. Is it because of the ordeal of the evening, or have I hurt you?" He still held my hand. "Trust me."

I couldn't tell him my feelings. He'd been so good to me and we had an understanding that we could never be close, because he was married. Dropping his hand, I stepped back, not wanting to bawl in front of him.

He stepped closer and put a soothing hand on my shoulder. "I am your friend, Janie. I will always love you that way—will always be grateful to you for all you've done, for loving my daughter and for treating my wife so kindly."

His touch felt more healing than I could have imagined. I leaned against his shoulder and began to cry, mixing all my raw emotions together: the trauma, the love lost, the loneliness, the lack of sleep.

After a few moments I gained my composure and moved away. "Good night," I said, wiping my tears with the back of my hand. "Thank you for the shoulder to cry on."

His eyes and his smile held regret, pain, relief, and joy, all mixed in one beautiful countenance. My heart swelled with love for him, a love I could never express.

A light caught my eye. In the open doorway to Roger's cottage stood his mother. She watched us, her face stern.

"Emily wanted to sleep in her own bed," I heard her say as Roger went in and closed the door.

Flo wagged her tail furiously and whimpered as I entered the apartment. I had been gone such a long time. I looked around the apartment and nothing was amiss. "Good girl!" I said as I locked the door behind me. After I dressed for bed, I said a prayer of thanks for our safety and crawled under the sheets. My female Marmaduke took her usual place at my feet, her presence bringing me a measure of peace.

I picked up the Book of Mormon on the bedside and read a verse or two, but I couldn't concentrate. I pushed away thoughts of Roger's healing touch. Then, I leaned back on the pillow and prayed, "Father, forgive me for loving such a wonderful man, and please help me get through this trial."

Soon, sleep came, easing my weary mind.

TWENTY-FIVE

"You never felt jealousy, did you, Miss Eyre? Of course not: I need not ask you; because you never felt love. You have both sentiments yet to experience: your soul sleeps; the shock is yet to be given which shall waken it."

I arrived at the police station the next morning, exhausted from staying up half the night. A specialist greeted me, and we sat at a computer where he used special software to put together a composite of the kidnapper. After I described the kidnapper's hair and the shape of his face, the specialist showed me a wide variety of each facial feature—eyes, eyebrows, nose, mouth, chin, and cheeks. All I had to do was select the image that best represented a particular feature in the kidnapper's face. In less than half an hour, a fair likeness of the kidnapper looked at me from the computer screen. It was more than a little eerie. Next, the specialist showed me the composite of Malinda he and Roger had created a month before. They still hadn't proven that she and the abductor worked together.

I arrived at the shop at noon. On the way from the police station, I'd called Jill to apologize for not showing up to flip pancakes at the breakfast with Santa. She'd assured me that plenty of parents had been eager to help.

Carmen and Cricket had opened the shop two hours earlier. As I walked in, I smelled roasting cacao beans and heard the *crunch* of the cracking machine, and I knew I'd be fine.

Carmen asked for a full rundown on the previous evening. I related the entire story up to, but not including, sobbing on Roger's shoulder. Then I told them my experience of sitting at the police station playing pick-the-facial-features-of-your-abductor with the police specialist.

"Thank goodness you two are safe!" Carmen exclaimed.

Cricket asked, "What was it like having a gun in your face?"

"Well, now I know what it's like to have my life pass before my eyes." It wasn't one of my most favorite memories. "It was about as fun as getting sick on a roller coaster."

I could barely stay awake as I worked in the kitchen, so I moved out to the store, hoping that helping customers would keep me alert. But after I dropped a chocolate rose on the floor, then did it again a few minutes later, Carmen encouraged me to go home before I doomed our profits.

"Well, I do have a few errands to run before I go home and sleep." I removed my apron.

"Don't worry. Cricket and I will stay until Tessa and Frank arrive." Carmen took my apron and hung it on the rack.

What amazing employees I have, I thought as I retrieved my purse. Just as I was starting out the back door, I heard the bell ring.

"Is Janie here?" I heard a woman ask Cricket.

I went into the shop. There stood Malinda, an intense look in her eyes. Cricket stayed to listen, or maybe to get ready to call the police—or the morgue. Malinda might kill one of them.

"I heard about Winnie's kidnapping on the news and came right away."

I didn't know if I should trust her, so I answered curtly, "I didn't think you would have to watch the news to know about it."

"I had nothing to do with it." Malinda sounded truly offended. "That is what I came to tell you."

"What about your friend?"

"Jack? He's in jail."

"No, the other man. The tattooed one—the one who was in the park during the murder. He kidnapped Winnie."

Malinda gasped. "I don't know who you're talking about. It was only Jack and me at the park." She stepped closer and banged her fist on the counter. "Listen. I expect Roger to think I know who kidnapped Winnie, or he'll tell the police I did it, but I had nothing to do with it. I don't know who did. Believe me."

She stared at me and our eyes locked. I hadn't expected her to be able to do that. Are liars supposed to be able to stare you in the eye?

"I will tell him," I said.

Malinda turned and marched out of the shop without looking back. Cricket gaped after her, speechless.

"Do you believe she doesn't know the kidnapper?" Carmen asked from the kitchen doorway.

"No. I'm sure she's lying." I turned to Carmen. "I still believe Roger's claim that two men left the park. If the kidnapper isn't one of them, who is he? The only reason

I'd believe Malinda is that she didn't seem to know the guy kidnapped me too."

"It could all be an act."

Cricket shuddered. "This is like something right out of *CSI*. Kind of spooky, if you ask me."

"The difference is we have no dead victim," I said. "Thank goodness!"

Everyone was silent, so I said, "Hey, Cricket. I haven't heard you hiccup yet today."

"Funny thing, I haven't hiccupped all day. I guess the trauma of last night cured me."

TWENTY-SIX

Her grave is in Brocklebridge churchyard: for fifteen years after her death it was only covered by a grassy mound; but now a grey marble tablet marks the spot, inscribed with her name, and the word "Resurgam."

The day of Linc's baptism arrived. We gathered on Friday afternoon at a stake center in Phoenix, and one of the full-time elders who had taught him performed the baptism. I had never seen Linc so happy. Dressed in white and with Jackie on his arm, he looked like an angel wearing cornrows and braids.

Jackie's family and Linc's mother and aunt attended the baptismal service. As I learned that evening, Jackie has three siblings and is the only Latter-day Saint in her family. She joined the Church about two years ago, and according to the elders, she is "on fire." Her parents have taken the missionary discussions but have not yet accepted baptism.

As a missionary gave a talk on baptism, I realized that if I had been asked six months ago which of all our employees would be baptized in the near future, I would never have chosen

Linc. I guess with the right encouragement by the right person, anyone with an open mind can come to see the truthfulness of the gospel.

Carmen, Cricket, and Bjorn also attended Linc's baptism. None of them is LDS, but they came to support Linc. Bjorn sat with his arm around Carmen through the entire service, though she still claimed they weren't dating. "He's just a very nice man," she insisted during refreshments of punch and chocolate cake, compliments of the shop. Willa and her tall, muscular date had dressed all in leather, since they planned to embark on a motorcycle adventure as soon as they left the church building.

I don't know why it surprised me when Carmen called late Monday evening. "I'm married," she announced. "I'm in Las Vegas!"

"Las Vegas?"

"Yep. It all happened so quickly. We just decided to get married, drove up, and here I am, Mrs. Bjorn Enevoldsen!"

"Well..." I was almost at a loss for words. "Congratulations! Does this mean you aren't coming into work tomorrow?"

"No, and not for the rest of the week. I hope you can get along without me."

I sighed, not wanting to get up before the roosters. "Take the week off. You don't get married every day." It was good of me, I know. Charity never faileth. "Have fun and say congratulations to Bjorn for me."

She repeated my words to her husband, then said goodbye. What a time to take a honeymoon with Christmas just around the corner! I shook my head and laughed. You just have to love Carmen!

I spent the next week getting up early to keep the chocolate-prep cycle going. In addition, I poured molds, baked cakes, and made the fudge. It was a lot of work! That's what I hired Carmen for, and I don't know how she does it. She's a redheaded wonder.

Kylee's birthday was in a few days. Her day sneaks up on me every year, and then I give her a card with an IOU. Tacky, I know. Kylee has come to expect it, which is the sad part. She always remembers my birthday and prepares ahead. She's so organized and thoughtful.

So, I decided to surprise her with a present on her actual birthday, thinking how fun it would be to see her face when she opened the box and found an actual present. The problem was, I didn't know what to get her. If she were a guy, I'd have bought a fishing pole or a tie, only because I have no imagination and because all men seem to have an occasion to go fishing and wear a tie—not at the same time, of course. The thought of it makes me snicker.

But I digress.

Anyone else could give a sister chocolate. All women love chocolate! In this case, I had a hunch chocolate wasn't the answer.

Getting Kylee what she wanted the most was out of the question. Besides, they don't sell babies at the mall. I had to think of another idea. After considering it a while, I realized if I chose for Kylee something I'd like myself, I probably couldn't go wrong. We were sisters, after all, so that gave us a lot in common. So, on this particular early-December pre-birthday day, I drove to Fiesta Mall to find the perfect gift.

I walked into the mall and was greeted by the sounds of thousands of shoppers. Christmas decorations draped the floor-to-ceiling corridor, and a fifty-yard-long line of excited children waited to meet Santa Claus. Festive music rang over the sound system, and the smell of food cooking and popcorn popping filled the air.

The Arizona Artists Art Gallery's window display caught my eye. I love art galleries, being somewhat of a sculptress myself—a sculptress in chocolate, that is.

Just for fun, I slipped into the quiet, softly lit shop. I noticed the smell of new carpet as I glanced around. The shop features many local artists, and the walls are filled with desert scenes and other typically Southwestern paintings.

My attention immediately went to a painting in oil that so beautifully captured the grandeur of an Arizona evening sky. An animate sunset dominated its canvas with fiery reds, yellows, and orange, in contrast to the dark, sleepy desert mountain range below. Curious, I looked at the label below the painting.

Winifred Wentworth, $5000.

Winnie! My knees almost buckled. Roger had told me his wife was an artist. Perhaps I'd seen and admired her paintings on display in the past—before I even met Roger.

"This painting is by local artist Winifred Wentworth. It is one of her best, and it is a numbered print." I turned to see the shop attendant standing behind me, dressed in a suit.

I examined the painting again. "It's beautiful. I love the colors."

"Yes. She has a unique style. This one you are looking at is one of her earlier paintings." He led me to another painting. "This is a later one. It has a different mood to it, wouldn't you say?"

He waited, clearly expecting an answer. "Yes, I—" I looked at the second painting. It was much darker, but still beautiful in its own right. Stormy skies crowded above purple mountains that towered over white fields of cotton that bent in the wind and rain.

"Amazing!" I breathed. "Please tell me what you know about her."

"Our company is her agent now that she is in poor health. I have met her on several occasions. I would say she is barely thirty—young for a successful artist. She showed great talent in her teens—mostly landscapes—but her talent is in capturing the true spirit of nature and then adding a touch of magic. Wouldn't you agree?"

"Absolutely." I turned back to the first painting. "It does have a touch of magic."

"I have a brochure about Ms. Wentworth." The salesman went to a desk and took the top brochure from a pile. I accepted it, thanked the salesman, and wandered out into the busy fairway of the mall.

I stopped and looked at the glossy brochure right there with a river of Christmas shoppers moving around me. It featured a glamour shot of Winnie, surrounded by several masterful paintings. It hadn't taken a lot to make her look glamorous. A light from behind created a halo around her dark hair,and her smile was as serene as I had seen it before. In the picture, however, her eyes had a presence that now seemed absent.

I stared at the portrait and Winnie stared back. *You have so much more going for you,* I found myself saying to her. *Beauty, talent, and the husband I would have picked for myself. An adorable daughter that I wish was mine.* Winnie only stared back, smiling at me. I slipped the brochure into my purse. *But I know you'd give up talent and fame for sanity.*

Coveting is one of the thou-shalt-nots in the Ten

Commandments. Here I stood, guilty. I would have to work on that some more.

I stopped to admire the Christmas display in another shop window. Among the holiday shoppers packing the store, one woman looked very familiar. I watched through the window for nearly half a minute to make sure. It was Malinda.

She stood before a three-fold mirror, modeling a shimmery peach-colored dress. I watched curiously. The gown had a braided empire waist and a pedal hemline. Its neckline was true to the plungers I had seen Malinda wear. She twirled to make the skirt flair. That's when I noticed the man who sat clapping his hands and encouraging her to twirl again.

I tried to get a better view, and even then, I could only see his dark blue pants and, once in a while, his hands and lower arms. Unfortunately, he wore long sleeves, so I couldn't tell if his arms were covered with tattoos. But my heart raced and I felt faint, terrified that he would see me. I told myself that I had to actually see his face before I called the police, so I slipped inside the store and tried to stay hidden from their view. I came as close as I dared, hiding behind a mannequin.

"Oh, Mike, will you buy the dress for me? I love it," Malinda exclaimed.

"Sure, baby doll," the man said. "You look like a dream."

"See? You do love me!"

"Never said I didn't. Want my baby doll to look good." He sounded like the man who had abducted Winnie and me, but I still wasn't certain.

I heard the smack of a quick kiss.

Okay, I made a mental note, *the man's name is Mike and he loves her, or at least she tries to convince herself he does.* I peeked out around the mannequin, but I couldn't see Mike's face. Then Malinda disappeared into the dressing room while he stayed in the chair. A thrill ran from my head to my toes as I realized I might catch her in her own lie.

I waited. Finally, Malinda came out of the dressing room carrying the dress on a hanger. The two walked past my hiding place. I turned my back and pulled a sweater from the clearance rack and held it up. Size 3X. Perfect to hide behind.

Mike and Malinda walked up to the checkout station. Malinda carefully draped the dress over the counter. I heard the register drawer open and pleasantries exchanged, but because Mike's back was to me, I couldn't see his face.

Mike had broad shoulders and a muscular build, similar to the kidnapper's. The suit he wore had more slimming lines than the Hawaiian shirt. From the back, he looked like a gangster straight out of a black-and-white movie, right down to his polished shoes.

"Come on, turn around so I can get a look at your face!" I mumbled impatiently.

Malinda slung the bagged dress over her shoulder and took Mike by the arm. They strolled out into the flow of people in the mall's corridor. I dodged other customers to reach the furthest display window to get a good look at Mike as he passed. I kept behind a lavender evening gown and had a perfect view.

He was the tattooed kidnapper!

I left the oversized sweater on a random rack, left the shop, and followed Mike and Malinda, staying far behind them. I dialed 911 on my cell phone and explained the situation to the dispatcher, giving her the history, the names, and every other bit of information I could think of, all while trying to keep Mike and Malinda in view.

The dispatcher said, "Don't let them out of your sight, but don't let them see you. Please stay on the line until the police arrive."

So I dodged shoppers and kept following with the cell phone to my ear. Malinda hung on the man's arm as they turned a corner leading to the parking lot. I quickened my pace, determined not to lose them. Move over Nancy Drew, here I come!

When I got to the corner, they were nowhere in sight. I went to the exit and looked through the glass, but they seemed to have vanished. "They're gone!" I cried out in dismay. *How did they get away so quickly?*

"Well, well. If it isn't Roger's girlfriend."

I whirled around and stood face to face with Malinda and Mike. His sinister chuckle made my skin crawl.

"Hello," Malinda said, grabbing my phone and closing it. As she dropped it into my purse, she saw the brochure I'd picked up at the art gallery. The photo of Winnie faced out. "What's this?"

Malinda yanked the brochure from my purse and studied it for a moment, then held it up for Mike to see.

He squinted at the picture, then chortled deep in his throat. "No wonder she lives in a fancy house. Roger's insane wife is famous." He stuffed the brochure in his pocket. I glared at him.

Malinda pointed toward Mike. "This is—uh—" She seemed to be at a loss for words.

"Mike," I filled in for her. Staring at his smirking, shaven face, I felt satisfied that the composite sketch did him justice.

I looked toward the mall exit, wondering what was taking the police so long. Then again, I didn't get a chance to tell the dispatcher where to find us. The officers were probably out there now, driving in circles. Why couldn't this have happened closer to a doughnut shop?

Mike nodded and his smirk turned foul. "We've met already," he said.

"Did you give Roger my message?" Malinda asked. She walked around back of me. They had me surrounded now and I tried to keep my eye on both of them.

"Not yet. I don't talk with him much," I answered.

Mike grinned and slipped his hand into his pocket. "We know better than that."

Remembering his gun, my heart raced. *Please, Heavenly Father, help me!* I prayed silently.

Malinda continued coolly, "Mike had nothing to do with the murder. Jack would have likely killed him too if I hadn't been waiting in the car." She stepped closer. "Convince Wentworth to drop his claim that he saw two men. Tell him to say he only saw Jack run away."

"That is a lie." I turned to look at Mike and his bulging pocket. "Mike isn't as innocent as you think. He's already guilty of kidnapping two people. And he took a shot at Roger. That's attempted murder."

Malinda looked shocked. "That shot was only a warning."

I stepped backward to face both of them. "Yeah, right. The police know better." Speaking of the police, where were they?

"Listen," Malinda growled, her calm demeanor gone. "We only want to live in peace. Jack is in jail, and he won't talk."

"Why won't he?"

"Mike knows too much about Jack that could damage him for life, so he won't."

"That's blackmail. Anyway, he's already in jail for murder."

"He'll get probation. He's claiming it was self-defense."

Mike took a step toward me. "Maybe kidnapping the lover again will get Wentworth to cooperate." He took hold of my arm and pulled out his gun.

"I—I'm not his lover." I saw the weapon and squirmed under Mike's grip. "I'm only a friend."

"Try convincing his wife of that," Mike sneered. "Winnie is crazy enough to believe anything. How about his mother? Wait until the heiress hears that her little boy is having an affair."

"Let go of me." I tried to yank my arm away from his viselike grip. "Why should anyone believe you, anyway?" I spat the words, but refrained from saying that Roger's mother already had her suspicions.

"People are gullible. They tend to believe the worst. You tell Roger that if he doesn't change his story, I will send letters, maybe to his boss too, but especially to his wife."

Four slouching, gangster-ish teenage boys, wearing sagging pants and tattoos, walked our way toward the exit. Mike let go of my arm and discreetly slipped the gun into his pocket. As the boys came closer, an idea came to me. I knew I'd be taking a big chance, maybe even putting innocent people in jeopardy, but I only had a few seconds to decide, and I was desperate. When the boys passed, I turned and fell into step with them, taking hold of the closest one's arm. "Hi, Sam! How is your sister doing?"

"Huh?" He looked at me as if I was crazy. I pulled him along without looking back.

"I haven't seen her for a few months. What's she been up to?" All I could really think of was the gun pointed at my back.

"My sister?"

As we continued toward the exit, I spoke through clenched teeth. "Stay with me and walk fast. Those people back there are harassing me." I looked back. Malinda stood with a dropped jaw and Mike looked madder than a hornet. My heart pounded. We pushed our way through the swinging glass doors.

The boy's face brightened. "Gotcha." He looked back. "You want us to go rough them up for ya?"

173

"No! No. The guy has a gun and I'd hate for someone to get hurt. Would one of you dial 911?"

"Cool!" The shortest boy pulled out a cell phone, dialed 911, and informed the operator of our location.

"This is like *America's Most Wanted* for real," my Sam said.

"Thanks for helping me get away from those two. You kids better go now," I said, concerned for their safety.

"Don't think we're gonna ditch you now. We'll at least wait until the cops get here," another of the boys said.

We didn't have to wait long. Two policemen arrived, parked at the curb, and headed toward the entrance. I turned back to look again, but Mike and Malinda were gone.

One officer went inside and the other came over to us. "Are you the ones who called?" he asked.

I told him what had happened. He listened, then stepped away from us and spoke into his walkie-talkie. Soon another police car arrived with two more officers.

"You kids wait for me at your car and keep away from the entrance," he instructed. "We have officers at each of the exits. The suspects won't be able to get out without us seeing them. I'll be back in a few minutes." We watched him go inside. The two other officers stood guard at the entrance doors.

We walked over to my car and leaned against it. One of the boys said, "You look very familiar to me, but I can't . . ." He raised an eyebrow. "Do you teach at the high school?"

"No, I own a chocolate shop in Tempe."

"Chocolate. Hmm. That's it!" He clicked his fingers and pointed. "You're Mrs. Arnold. You came to the school and brought chocolate turkeys."

I laughed, which relieved the tension a bit. "Mrs. Arnold is my sister."

"Those turkeys were *suh-weet!*"

"Thanks. I helped make them."

"Mr. Arnold is our weight-training coach."

Then I did what I usually do in a moment of stress. I called Kylee. Jim answered the phone.

"I have four of your students with me," I repeated their names as they gave them: Cort, Rex, Tim, and Kevin. I told Jim about the conversation with Mike and Malinda. "And these young men were ready to go back there and rough them up for me."

"They probably would have, too," Jim responded. "No—they are good guys even though they look odd." I heard, in the background, one of his girls asked him a question. "Do you need me to come?" he asked me. "I'm babysitting, so I'd have to bring the kids."

"No need to come. These boys say they will stay with me."

They all nodded.

"We like being part of the excitement," Cort said toward the cell phone so Jim could hear.

After what seemed like an hour, the officer returned and took our statements. Then he told us to go home.

"Come by the shop sometime," I told the boys, "and I'll give you a treat for helping me." I took out my Chocolate Art Forever business card and handed one to each boy. "You guys really saved me today!"

"No problem," Rex said.

"Later," Tim called as the boys walked away, looking happy with their tickets to some free chocolate.

Relieved the ordeal was over, I got in my car, certain the police would find Mike and Malinda and put them in jail. But as I turned onto Southern Avenue, I remembered I still didn't have a birthday present for Kylee.

TWENTY-SEVEN

His language was torture to me; for I knew what I must do—and do soon—and all these reminiscences, and these revelations of his feelings only made my work more difficult.

Like a Houdini act, Mike and Malinda had disappeared from the mall. After searching every nook of the mall, including every dressing room, the police gave up their search.

I gave Kylee the traditional IOU for her birthday. She didn't seem surprised. I promised to do better at Christmas.

Carmen and Bjorn returned from their honeymoon acting like newlyweds. (Guess that's no surprise, huh?) I will spare you the details; just know the rest of us rolled our eyes a lot. But it was good to see Carmen so happy.

Our routine in the shop returned to normal, as normal as it gets during the holidays. Personally, I was relieved that Carmen had returned—literally relieved from having to keep such early hours. She resumed coming in to make the chocolate, but her dance had changed. No longer did she hula around the kitchen; instead, she did something more like a polka.

School let out for the holidays, so Cricket worked in the shop in the mornings with me while Kylee stayed home with her children and balanced the books. We used all our holiday molds, including complete Nativity sets. We even created a Nativity set to display in our glass cabinet. The set included Joseph and Mary, and of course, Baby Jesus lying on chocolate-covered pretzel sticks in a fudge manger under a milk chocolate star, surrounded by a complete cast of molded chocolate sheep, shepherds, and angels. Customers who had purchased Nativity sets the year before returned to buy them again.

I had started wiping off the kitchen counters when I heard Cricket laughing. "What are you guys doing here?"

Her question piqued my interest, so I tossed aside the rag and stepped into the shop just in time to see my four teenage rescuers from the mall toss their Chocolate Art Forever cards onto the counter and say, "Janie invited us."

"Janie?" Cricket turned to me and questioned, "You know these guys?"

"I sure do!" They hadn't changed at all; they still wore baggy shorts around their hips and long T-shirts. "These are my friends from the mall."

"Really? Do you know who these guys are?" she gushed.

I looked over the young men. Obviously "friends from the mall" was the wrong answer. They grinned and looked at me expectantly.

"No. Who are they?" I asked finally.

"They are FOUR MORE," Cricket replied, "only the hottest hip-hop dance team on campus—probably the whole city. I mean, probably the whole state, and probably—"

"You guys are a dance team?" I interrupted.

They nodded and kept smiling.

"But how do you dance? Don't your pants fall off?"

"Show her, guys." Cricket said.

Without hesitation, the boys pushed the parlor tables out of the way. One of the boys pulled out his iPhone and started some music, then set it on a table. In unison, they pulled their pants to their waists and connected two belt loops with a carabiner. Then the boys started dancing in precision.

With my mouth open in amazement, I watched these tattooed, wild-looking juveniles put on an incredible performance. Their kicks were in flawless unison. They rolled their heads together in perfect timing, and they twirled with exactness. And their pants stayed up.

With the last note as our cue, Cricket and I applauded. "Great show!" I said. "Would you guys come back in two weeks? We're having a wedding party for an employee— Cricket's mother, in fact—who recently got married. Will you come dance?"

The boys agreed happily and gave me a contact number. Cricket and I loaded them up with chocolate before they left.

We held the party celebrating the Enevoldsens' marriage on a Saturday night. In spite of Carmen changing her dance, we served the chocolate hula dancer from the mold I designed for the occasion. My next creation would be something Scandinavian, I decided.

Linc brought his Jamaican steel band from campus and they set up on the sidewalk in front of the store. Since it was only a few days until Christmas, they played familiar carols—with upbeat Jamaican rhythms, of course. FOUR MORE showed up and danced until they were exhausted. Jim, Kylee, and the kids came, and of course, Tessa and Frank worked the counter. We all had a great time, even Cricket. (By the way, her hiccupping problem permanently disappeared after the kidnapping. Go figure. She says she's keeping her name anyway.)

On Monday morning, a call came for me on the shop's business line. We were crazily busy, with customers lined up halfway to the door.

"Go ahead and take the call in the office," Kylee said, stepping up to fill the order I was working on.

I hurried into the office and picked up the phone. "This is Pam Wentworth, Roger's mother," said the acidic voice on the line. "I received the most disturbing letter today stating that you and my son Roger are having an affair. Winnie received one too, and it has nearly destroyed her. I demand to know if the accusation is true."

My blood flow went into hyper drive. I could hardly breathe. "It isn't true. I promise," I managed to say. "Roger is being blackmailed into changing his story about the murder."

"He claims the same, but I don't know what is true. He's with Winnie right now trying to calm her."

"Believe your son. He's a good man, and he's trustworthy." A ripple of discomfort went through me as I remembered seeing her standing in Roger's doorway after the kidnapping. "We are only friends. Please believe me."

"I wanted to hear you deny these allegations. Of course I've seen you together, so I figured there might be some truth to it." She paused and I heard her huff. "Janie, I will give you one last chance to tell the truth. Roger is married. His wife is very ill and the thought of him carrying on an affair is killing her."

"Then assure her that she has nothing to fear. Roger has told her that already, I'm sure. He's as faithful to her as Adam was to Eve."

"Yes," the woman said, "and a serpent came between them."

The phone went silent. I stared at the receiver for a moment. "Well, you have a happy Christmas too," I mumbled, then slowly put down the receiver. Clearly, there was nothing more I could've said to assure the woman.

The head of TriCorp Airlines received a duplicate letter. Roger told me about it that evening when I ran into him in the courtyard. Discussing our alleged affair was beyond awkward, but I was relieved to hear the TriCorp executives hadn't taken the letter seriously. Roger explained that rumors about employees often circulated around the company, and they got a crackpot letter at least once a year. Luckily, they took this one as such.

Winnie was the one I worried about. Roger said she didn't say a word during and after his explanation about the letter, so he couldn't tell what she was thinking. She had often refused to discuss an issue, reacting only with cold silence, but later threw fits over it. Roger feared the volcano was yet to erupt.

Flo and I spent Christmas Day with Kylee, Jim, and the kids. Aunt Lucy flew into Arizona on her way back from helping with earthquake cleanup in some country I'd never heard of, long enough to spend the day with us too. We laughed, ate good food, played games, and read the Christmas story from the Bible. I felt much better, realizing again that I wasn't alone and that I was blessed with a great family who loves me and stands with me through the hard times. The next day, Aunt Lucy flew off to somewhere in the Pacific, to help clean up after a hurricane.

I didn't see Roger or Emily during the holidays except at church on Sunday.

A few days after Christmas, Flo and I spent a quiet evening at home coming down from all the excitement. We munched on stale cookies and dog biscuits, and I took the ornaments off our tiny tree and packed them carefully in a storage box. I must have still been a tad wired, because I jumped when my cell phone rang. I said hello cautiously.

"Hi, Janie. This is John. Merry Christmas!"

I sighed with relief, glad it wasn't Mike or Malinda.

"Hi, John. Has it been a month already?" I had hardly missed him, with Christmas and my busy schedule. I expected he'd called to schedule our monthly date, so I lied. "My calendar is pretty full."

"I'd like to drop by tonight because I have some good news that can't wait. It includes you, too."

Me? I glanced at my watch—9:00 PM. "All right." What kind of good news needed announcing so late at night? Was he getting baptized into the LDS Church?

I put on a sweater and moved out to the lawn chair so we wouldn't be alone in my apartment. Of course, I brought Flo along to chaperone.

John arrived within minutes, and I invited him to sit on the grass. Something seemed different about him, but I waited until he spoke.

"I have taken a job," he announced proudly.

"A job?" I waited for him to continue but he didn't, so I urged him on. "Good. What is it?"

"I'm going to India to be a missionary."

I stared. I knew he was a set-in-his-ways Baptist, but a missionary? "Wow," I said, trying to sound enthusiastic. "India is far away."

"Why are you surprised? You Mormons go on missions all the time."

"I know, but our missions are a bit different. They aren't jobs so we don't get paid. In fact, we pay our own way."

John batted my comment aside. "The good news is, I'm taking you with me. The council said it would be advantageous if I were married, and that a wife would bring me more respect as I preach liberty to them that are enslaved."

(Now say that last line with the zeal of a Southern preacher and you'll hear it the way I heard it.)

John stared at me with the same expectant smile Flo wears while waiting for me to throw a ball. I couldn't speak. My brain buzzed. I felt like I was dreaming, and it wasn't a pleasant dream. At last, I found my tongue. "John, is this a proposal?"

"Of course!" He still wore that goofy smile. "Janie, come with me to India. Come as my helpmeet and fellow laborer."

My first proposal. It wasn't anything like I'd imagined. Where were the roses, the ring, and the chocolate? Where was the guy I actually loved, or could at least stand to be around?

"What does your heart say?" he asked overdramatically.

"John, I'm not marrying you, if marriage is what you mean."

"God and nature intended you for a missionary's wife. I claim you—not for my own pleasure, but for my Sovereign's service."

In disbelief, I stared. "You are a nut. You take me out once a month, you don't even call me on Christmas, and now you think I will jump up and marry you? What kind of duo would a Mormon and a Baptist be, anyway?"

"Well rounded." He smiled again.

"I'd be organizing a dance while you were out preaching against it."

"My dear" —he covered his heart as if protecting it— "do not be silly. There will be no dancing."

I started to get angry. "And what kind of proposal is this? You are demanding rather than proclaiming love."

He looked at me in obvious confusion. "If my lack of presentation is what's bothering you—" He knelt on one knee and put his hands together as if begging. He looked so ridiculous that my anger subsided and I had to stifle a laugh.

"Janie, will you go with me to India as my missionary companion and marry me first to make our living together legal?"

At that moment, Roger's door opened. I glanced over at him. He stared at us. John held his pose and looked at me confidently.

Roger looked stunned. "I'm sorry. I didn't mean to interrupt." He stepped back and closed the door.

Humiliated, I jumped out of the chair, and although I wanted to shout, I tried to keep my voice low. "John, I'm not marrying you. I'm not going to India to be a Baptist missionary. This whole thing is ridiculous." I looked over at Flo. She snoozed soundly—so much for a chaperone!

John stood too. "What?" Now he looked even more confused.

"I said no."

"But I—" He ran his hand through the few strands of blond hair on his balding head. "I was sure you'd—"

I turned his teddy-bear body in the direction of his car. "And the next time you propose to a girl, get on your knee without being prompted. Don't forget the ring, the roses, or the chocolate." I patted his shoulder and gave him a gentle shove. "Best wishes in India."

He staggered through the gate and toward his car parked

on the street. As he walked around to the driver's side he mumbled, "But I . . . "

I saluted like a sailor. "It's been nice knowing you."

He got in his car and drove slowly to the corner, then squealed the tires as he made the turn onto LeSueur Street. I stood there long after he'd gone.

A proposal! Not much of one, but real. Roger peeked through the curtains. I waved and then nudged Florentine. "Wake up, lady. You had the chance of a lifetime to go to India, and you slept through it."

TWENTY-EIGHT

On that same occasion I learned . . . that my father had been a poor clergyman; that my mother had married him against the wishes of her friends, who considered the match beneath her.

Sunday after church, April shoved a flyer into my hand. "This is the Young Adult's New Year's party. I hope you can go." She smiled sweetly and I read in her eyes that she thought me old enough to date her grandfather.

You would think I would've learned my lesson about Young Adult dances, but I was at a disadvantage because I wasn't a member of a singles ward. I'd kind of fallen out of the loop of activities where a girl might meet eligible bachelors.

Anyway, I don't know why I ended up at that dance. The committee had cleverly decorated the indoor basketball courts with pine trees hanging by wires from the rafters. The hall had a magical feeling, like an enchanted forest. Maybe this was my lucky night to meet my Prince Charming.

I only knew a few people in the crowd besides the girls from my last singles ward, whom I stood talking with in a circle.

Guess who walked up to me?

"Hi, Santa Fe," Trevin said. He smiled and looked at each of my friends, nodding in greeting. I wondered if I owed him the honor of introductions, but decided no. "You wouldn't like to dance, would you?" He grabbed my arm and pulled me around a few trees to the dance floor.

It was a slow song from the '70s. At least he knew to put his hand on my waist and hold up his other hand for me to take. "Hey, Santa Fe," he said again after a full minute, his attention anywhere in the room but on me. "I've been thinking. Since we both are still around and no one else has wanted to marry us, maybe we ought to think about getting married."

I stepped back and dropped his hand. "To each other?" He nodded. The magical spell of the fairy tale forest must have gone to his head. "What is this, a marriage proposal?" I put my hands on my hips and lifted an eyebrow, awaiting his reply.

"Not actually a marriage proposal. It's a . . . I don't know . . . a suggestion? We're both leftovers, you know."

I knew, but I wasn't about to spend the rest of my life listening to Trevin's uncultured remarks, or trying to culture him for that matter, only to have a husband. "No," I said. Wow! My second marriage proposal/refusal within the week.

"Just consider it," he said with a shrug. Then he backed into a tree, spun around to recover himself, and walked away, leaving me on the dance floor. The song was only halfway over. Perturbed, I wandered back to my circle of friends. It was all I could do not to walk out and go home that very minute.

"Who was that guy you danced with?" the girl standing next to me asked with wide eyes. She glanced toward Trevin, now half hidden behind a tree.

I searched my brain to remember her name but couldn't. "Oh, he's a guy from my home ward. Trevin Worliss."

"He's so cute!" she gushed. I turned to look objectively at Trevin.

He actually is good looking, but he is missing some sort of coolness link, an absence that to me makes him rather, well, unattractive. But I figured if this girl was attracted to him, why should I stand in their way of happiness because of a minor detail?

"Would you like me to introduce you to him?" I asked with all the kindness I could muster.

Her eyes widened even more. "Yes!"

We made our way over to Trevin while I dug even further into my memory for her name, but with no luck. "Uh, Trev. My friend wants to meet you."

He looked at her and smiled. I said to her, "This is Trevin Worliss from Wickenburg, and this is . . ."

"Tedi Campbell," she said before I made up a name. "Hi." She put out her hand and giggled.

After the introduction, they started talking, so I left and went back to my circle. Trevin and Tedi. You can't get much cutesier than that.

The next song was a rock rendition of "Some Enchanted Evening."

A customer had given me two tickets to the Phoenix Zoo, so I arranged to take Thursday afternoon off work to go. Remembering how thrilling the zoo was for me as a child, I looked around for the nearest four-year-old, and *voila!* I found Emily. So, earlier in the week, I went to her door to invite her to come along, even though Roger wasn't supposed to be talking to me. Fortunately, he gave his permission.

"Are you getting married?" he asked hesitantly before I left.

"Married?" I had to drag John's proposal from my memory, and then Trevin's. Had he heard about that one too? No way. "Oh, yeah. John. Well, I told him no."

"You said no? I didn't think Mormon girls were supposed to do that," Roger joked.

"John is a nice man, but he's a Baptist and wanted me to accompany him on his mission to India. You think I should have said yes to such a proposal?"

"Maybe. You'd get to see the Taj Mahal." Roger smiled, and the relief in his eyes surprised me.

Emily and I had a blast looking at lions, bears, and all the lizards and snakes we'd ever want to see. The Phoenix Zoo has the latter two in abundance. There are mountain goats, komodo dragons, and lots of other animals I can't remember now. (I'd hate to be an exotic animal people couldn't remember.)

It was a fun, exhausting day—exhausting because I had a hard time keeping up with Emily and all her energy. When I thought I couldn't walk any farther because of my aching muscles, I bought popcorn and we sat on the grass under a shady tree. Yes, we have a few shady trees in Arizona. And some grass, too.

Emily lay back on the grass and looked up into the tree. "Janie, if a genie gave you a wish, what would you ask for?" She stuffed a few kernels of popcorn in her mouth.

I wondered if she had recently watched the movie *Aladdin*. It seemed a deep question for such a small person.

"I guess I would wish for a tall, handsome husband who loved chocolate, big dogs, and didn't mind hips." I left out the part about her dad being tall and handsome, and that in my past life, I had spent many wishes on him but only lacked a genie. "What would you wish for?"

"That my daddy and me could go live with Mama, and Mama could be well and be nice again." I wasn't surprised at her answer. Emily sat up. "But then I wouldn't see Flo every day."

"We could visit once in a while." I tried to toss a few kernels of popcorn and catch them in my mouth, but I missed. (Everyone's a kid at the zoo.) A flock of pigeons immediately swooped down to fight over the kernels.

Emily lay back on the grass again. "I'd like that. I would miss Flo a whole bunch."

"How often do you get to see your mother?" I tried the tossing thing and missed again.

"Oh," she shrugged, "not very often. She isn't well. She's angry a lot."

I tried to think of how to explain it all to Emily. How Winnie feels isn't anyone's fault; it's probably a genetic disorder. Was it my place to try to explain that to the child? I decided it wasn't.

I had rested long enough and felt like trekking on. "Let's go see the giraffes, and then go get ice cream."

We arrived home after Roger did. When he opened the door, I said, "Thank you for letting her go with me. We had a great time."

"We saw giraffes and a dragon." Emily said, marching into the apartment and dropping her souvenir gorilla hat on the couch. She immediately spun around. "Can I go see Flo? She has missed me all day."

It was probably the truth.

Emily led the way to my door and as soon as I unlocked it, Flo bounded out and circled the courtyard. In minutes, the two were rolling on the lawn.

"What's this about a dragon?" Roger asked from beside me.

I hadn't expected him to follow since we had said goodbye—twice now.

"Komodo dragon," I answered, too aware that he stood close now. I remembered the brotherly comfort he'd given me a month before, and the same feelings came back. *This is not good,* I thought. *Whatever happened to moving on?*

"We had fun," I said, taking a short step away. "Emily is a natural at imitating monkeys."

He grinned. "She isn't imitating. She *is* one."

Emily ran to her father, with Flo right behind. Emily hugged Roger's leg. "Daddy! Janie said she would take me to see Mama tomorrow. Can she, Daddy? I promise to be good."

He shot a glance my direction, then ruffled her curls. "I don't think so, princess."

"Please? She promised."

He looked at me again.

"I promised," I said.

"Winnie hasn't blown up over the letter yet, but I'm sure it's coming." He paused for a moment, then sighed. "I suppose it will be all right. I shouldn't keep Emily away from her mother. But Janie, I think it's best if you stay in the car and keep it a short visit. That's all Winnie can handle. When I stay too long, I'm reminded all too well of why we don't live together."

TWENTY-NINE

While I paced softly on, the last sound I expected to hear in so still a region, a laugh, struck my ears. It was a curious laugh—distinct, formal, mirthless.

Emily danced excitedly when I told her I'd pick her up at the sitter's at noon to take her to see her mother.

The sitter, a pretty, blonde woman named Becky, runs a daycare in her well-kept home. When I arrived, four bouncing children briefly stopped to see who had walked in. I knew right then where Emily had nurtured her monkey abilities.

Roger called Winnie's caregiver to tell her what time we would arrive. I took along *Chocolate Lover's Magazine* to read in the car while Emily went in to visit.

At the gate, I pressed the intercom button and Grace's voice answered, "Yes?"

"I brought Emily to see Winnie."

"There's Mama!" Emily squealed from the back seat.

I looked toward the lawn and saw Winnie sitting on a chair

at an easel, holding a palette. The setting made a lovely picture, and I shrank, realizing again what a beautiful woman she was—and how, in comparison, I was plain. The gate opened and I drove the car up to the front porch, and then the gate automatically closed.

"Mama! Mama!" Emily squealed again. I heard the click of her seatbelt as it freed her. "Open the door, Janie. I want to go to Mama!"

The only way to for me to open the door was to get out and open it from the outside. I had originally planned to walk Emily to the door and then come back to my car, but here, with Winnie outdoors, I'd be in plain sight.

"Hurry!" Emily squealed. I got out and opened the car door, keeping my face hidden as much as possible. Emily leaped from the car and ran across the plush grass to her mother. Winnie put down the palette just in time to catch her daughter as Emily jumped into her arms. Their long hair tumbled over one another. It was as heartwarming as anything on the big screen, only genuine.

What is more beautiful than a mother and daughter reunited and so happy to see one another? Of course I was happy for them, yet I also felt a twinge of jealousy. I climbed back into my SUV, rolled down the window, and hid my face in the magazine.

I couldn't concentrate and had to peek at Winnie and Emily. The little girl had been, in my eyes, all mine. This was the first time I had seen her with Winnie. I reminded myself that they were a family—Roger, Winnie, and Emily—and I was the outsider. In this private little haven hidden from the world behind a tall fence and leafy shrubs, I was an intruder in an intimate moment between Emily and her mother, even though I had sort of made that moment possible. I tried to pull my mind from the scene and force myself to look at the magazine.

I heard Winnie ask, "Who brought you here, Emily?"

I turned my back toward the car window as best I could.

"It's Janie. She's in the car."

The two walked across the grass and I heard Winnie say, "Hello, Janie." She sounded rather confused by my presence. "Are you delivering chocolate today?"

I wanted to climb in the back seat and hide, but instead I turned around and opened the door. "Hello, Winnie!" I laughed stiffly as I climbed out of the vehicle. "No chocolate today. I brought Emily to visit you."

"Where is Roger?" Winnie asked.

"He's working."

"Janie took me to the zoo yesterday!" Emily reported with excitement. "We saw monkeys and elephants and ate popcorn."

At Winnie's cross look, I smiled guiltily. She pulled Emily closer to her and I could see the wheels turning in her pretty head. Her serene countenance changed to an enraged one. "My daughter?" She spit the words. "My husband?"

An alarm went off in my head, and I knew I'd rather be anywhere but standing in that driveway at the moment. Deep, dark Africa would have been better. I took a few awkward steps toward the house. "I'll go in and talk with Grace," I said, knowing I had nothing specific to say to the nurse, and headed for the front door.

"Stay here and let's talk this out!" Winnie called after me. She sounded desperate. She sounded angry. She sounded way past meds time.

I stopped to face her. "We have nothing to talk about." Ignoring the pang of shame inside me, I tried to sound sweet and innocent.

Anger flashed in Winnie's haunted eyes. "Why are you taking my family away from me?"

I took another step toward the house. I suspected my bright red cheeks made me look even guiltier. "I—I'm not taking your family from you. I only help Roger with Emily when he needs me. Like today." *And yesterday. And last month.* "I own a Great Dane that is Emily's best friend."

"Best friends with a dog?" Winnie looked horrified and pulled Emily closer.

Emily looked at me, her eyes pleading for help. Then she turned to her mother. "She's a nice dog. Her name is Flo."

Winnie glared at me, not loosening her grip on her daughter. "I know what you are doing. You want to take Emily away from me. You've already taken Roger. He is in love with you, isn't he? And with me locked up in here—how convenient! I got a letter from a man telling me you two were having an affair. Roger tried to deny all of it, but I knew better."

She let go of Emily, took a step, and lunged toward me with her manicured nails. In self-defense, I caught hold of her arms and pushed her. She crumpled to the ground and started to cry. Of course, I was horrified.

Emily rushed to her side and tried to hug her. "Mama! Don't be mad. Be happy. Be happy!"

"Winnie, I'm so sorry," I said sincerely. "It's not the way you think at all. Believe me. Please."

I placed my hand on her shoulder where she sat on the ground, but she recoiled and whipped around. "Don't touch me, you family breaker! You husband stealer!" she screamed. "I hate you! Leave my house!" Tears came, causing her mascara to run. "Just go. Go now!"

I took a step backward, then another, not knowing what to do. I couldn't leave Emily. The little girl stood, her face showing the quandary she felt. Should she follow her friend or stay with her mother?

Fortunately, at that moment, Grace came from the house. "Winnie? Are you all right?" She glanced toward me. "What happened?" Then going to Winnie, she took her gently by the shoulders.

"Maybe we should come back another day," I said.

Grace nodded. "Let's go inside now, Winnie." Winnie relaxed at the woman's touch. "Say goodbye to Emily."

Clearly bewildered, Emily hugged her mother. Then Grace helped Winnie to stand. The nurse turned to me and sighed. "Another incident I need to report to the caseworker."

She grasped Winnie by the arm and guided her toward the house. Winnie hung her head in defeat. "There, there, Winnie," Grace said soothingly. "Everything will be all right."

Dazed at the sudden anger and then the almost immediate surrender, I could only watch until the two women went inside and closed the door.

Emily came to me and took my hand. We walked in silence to the car. I buckled her into the child's seat and we quietly drove away.

"My mother isn't well," came a tiny voice from the back seat after we had been driving for a few minutes. I glanced up at Emily's cherubic face in my rearview mirror and wondered how many outbreaks she had witnessed in her short life, and like today, how many times she had tried to be the peacemaker.

"Your mother is a good woman and she loves you very much."

Emily nodded and thought for a moment. "Are you going to be my other mother?"

Caught off guard, I searched for the right words. "Emily, I will always be here for you whenever you need me. Flo will always be your friend too. And Winnie will always be your mother. She'll get well someday. Just wait. The doctors will find the right medicine, and then she will be just like she used to be."

"My daddy will always be my daddy."

"Yes, your daddy is a good father. You have a lot of people who love you."

I glanced again in the mirror at Emily, who gazed out the window. She had been told so many times that Winnie would get well—so many that she had probably become numb to it.

"Grandma. And Flo."

I smiled. "Yes. Flo is one of the most loving people I know." Being almost human, Flo qualified.

My heart ached for Emily. I would make good on my word to always be there for her, but that meant I would regularly see Roger for the next several years. He and I had already said goodbye and it was more for my good, I'm sure, than his. Would I come to a point where I could think of Roger platonically?

Yes. For Emily, I had to.

When we arrived at my cottage, Roger was still at work. Our visit had been brief, as Roger had requested, then cut even shorter by poor Winnie's episode. Emily stayed at my apartment and played with Flo until the three of us fell asleep on the bed, Emily and I both emotionally drained. Hanging halfway off the bed, Flo snoozed contentedly.

I awoke to a soft knock on the door. When I opened it, there stood Roger, looking tired but as handsome as ever. I held my tongue so as not to dump the events of the day on him, which I really wanted to do.

"Is Emily still here?" He peeked around me. "How did the visit go with her mother?"

I opened my mouth to dump, but Emily came yawning from the bedroom, Flo following. The child climbed into Roger's arms when he stooped to greet her, and then she started crying. He frowned and looked at me, clearly expecting an explanation.

"Our visit didn't turn out happy—at all."

Roger raised an eyebrow. "Oh?"

"Mama was angry." Emily sniffled and put both arms around his neck. "She said Janie was stealing us."

He looked at me. I nodded. "Shall we discuss this later?" he asked.

"All right."

He turned to go but Emily suddenly cried, "I have to say goodbye to Flo!" The little girl wiggled from her father's arms and gave the dog a hug. "I'll see you later, Flo."

As Roger and Emily left my cottage and stepped onto the grass, he pulled a wrinkled, folded piece of paper from his pants pocket. He held it out to me. "Look what was on my door when I got home."

I pulled the door closed behind me, though Flo had escaped to follow her little friend. Trying to conceal a sigh, I stepped off the porch, took the paper, and unfolded it. It didn't look much different than a fortune-cookie note, but the message was haunting.

YOUR LITTLE ONE IS NEXT.

"No! They wouldn't." Looking past Roger to Emily, who now played noisily with Flo on the lawn, I felt an overwhelming love for the little girl and a desire to protect her. I handed the note back to Roger.

"They would." He stuffed the note into his pocket again. "The police know his first name, and if he is the same crook they think he is, they know that Jack is only his pawn. Mike is wanted for extortion and is a suspect in two other murders."

Roger's words gave me chills. I had been held at gunpoint by a murderer! "Then, please, lock your doors and don't let Emily out of your sight."

Roger searched my face as if looking for a better answer. The worry in his eyes—a very tired worry—told me he'd had enough of this watching-over-your-shoulder stuff. He shrugged. "I'll have to take her away from here. I don't think they'd do anything tonight, since they want to give me time to change my story, but maybe I should start looking for another place to live—somewhere they wouldn't look for us."

"Where? A monastery? They'll find you there too."

He dug his hands into his pockets and smiled. "A nunnery, then?"

"Let Emily stay with me tonight," I offered.

Roger turned serious again and took a deep breath. I knew he was considering the idea. "No," he said, "I want to keep her close." He turned to his daughter. "Let's go home and get some dinner, princess."

Emily stood. "I'm teaching Flo to shake hands. Watch." She offered her hand to the dog, who lifted hers for a handshake. Flo looked at me, clearly wanting praise. That little sneak! She learned to shake hands a long time ago.

"Good girl!" I said, playing along.

Roger turned to me. "When I get home, I'll call the sergeant and tell him about the note. Maybe he'll order more patrols in our area."

Flo and I watched father and daughter walk across the courtyard to their apartment. I heard him turn the locks once they were inside.

The rest of the evening was uneventful compared to the day's events—not that I'd want to repeat any of it. I sat in the living room and tried to read, but I ended up just listening for anyone entering the courtyard. Occasionally, I parted the curtains to peek out. Everything seemed quiet and peaceful.

I went to bed earlier than usual and would have slept soundly if Flo hadn't hogged more than her share of the bed. At about 1:00 AM, a frantic pounding startled us awake. Flo went to the door while I pulled on a robe. I listened before asking, "Who is it?"

"Janie, it's Roger."

Roger! Oh, no! Had something happened to Emily? The locks seemed stubborn as I clumsily fumbled with the top latch, then the deadbolt and the knob. I flung open the door to see Roger holding Emily, wrapped in a blanket and cradled in his arms. I sighed with relief, but Roger appeared troubled. Though he was fully dressed, his shirt hung open, exposing the scooped neck of his undergarments and the top part of his bare chest.

"What's wrong?" I asked.

"I need to leave. There's trouble at my wife's house. Will you keep Emily?"

"Sure, but what's happened?" I stepped over the threshold to take the sleeping child, but he held to her.

"I'd feel better not leaving her here, not after the note today. Please take her to my mother's or to Kylee's." He seemed anxious to leave. "Let me put her in your car." He turned toward the parking lot.

I pulled my robe securely around me, grabbed my keys and cell phone off the table in one swipe, and headed across the lawn while fumbling with the remote to my SUV. Finally, I pushed button and the locks released. Roger opened the door and laid his daughter on the back seat, then closed the door quietly.

"Take her away from here, please." He headed toward his car.

"Wait! Give me your mother's phone number so I can warn her we're coming." He quoted it so quickly that I could hardly program my phone fast enough. He got into his car and backed quickly out of the reserved space, the tires spinning in the gravel. In seconds, Roger was speeding down the street.

All was quiet again as I looked at the beautiful sleeping child in the back seat of my car. The whole scene had happened so fast that I had to take a moment to catch my breath. Flo came to my side, looking up at me as if wondering what to do next.

The lights went on in Sister Carter's apartment. Then the door opened. "Janie? What is going on?" she called.

"I'm not sure, but I have to leave. Would you watch my car while I get what I need from my apartment? Emily Wentworth is asleep in the back seat. Please, don't let her out of your sight."

Mrs. Carter agreed. What a blessing! Dressed in a thin, pink nightgown, she shuffled out into the chilly night in her fluffy slippers, then stood in a spot where she could see my car. Back in my apartment, I pulled on a pair of jeans, traded my nightgown for a T-shirt, and stuffed clothes and things I would need later into an overnight bag. After locking the door, I went to Roger's, and, using his key to enter (no time for sappy thoughts), I grabbed some clothes for Emily.

"Thank you so much for your help, Sister Carter." In spite of my load, I gave the shivering woman a brief hug. "Now get inside before you freeze to death." I tossed the clothes into the back of the SUV, let Flo in, and started to get into the driver's seat.

Mrs. Carter still waited. "Where are you headed? What's going on?" she asked.

"Roger said something about trouble at his wife's house. I'm sure he'll be able to take care of it. I'm taking Emily to her grandmother's. Oh!" I wanted to retract my words. "Please, Sister Carter, if anyone comes around asking where we went, please don't tell them—no matter who they are."

She looked surprised. "All right." She didn't press for information but only waved goodbye. I waited in the car until she went into her apartment. Praying for the dear woman's safety, I backed my vehicle out of the parking space.

Flo crouched in the cargo compartment and whimpered with her chin on the seat, looking down at Emily.

"Now's no time to play," I told her. "Be a good girl and let Emily sleep." Flo obeyed with a sigh, turning to curl up on the floor. Sometimes I think my dog's IQ is higher than that of some humans I know.

"Should we go to Kylee's?" I asked my intelligent canine. "I'm sure she'll love us waking her in the middle of the night. But I'd rather not face Roger's mother."

As always, the temple lights glowed. I drove north to Brown Road and then headed east toward my sister's house.

Even with few cars on the road, I hit every light on red. Clearly, I didn't have Roger's good fortune with traffic lights. Getting annoyed with playing Red Light, Green Light, I looked in my rearview mirror to see a fire truck wailing up behind me. Immediately, I pulled to the side of the road. One, two, three fire trucks passed by. *A slow night,* I thought sarcastically. Then the trucks turned onto Val Vista and a sickening feeling washed over me. I looked north. Smoke billowed above the trees, and the night sky glowed red. What were the odds the fire was at Roger's house?

Curiosity compelled me to turn onto Val Vista. The farther north I drove, the brighter the horizon glowed and the more certain my fears became. On the same block as Roger's house, police cars lined the streets and emergency lights flashed. Fire trucks occupied the center of the road. My heart did a sick flip and I fought the urge to throw up. Slowing the car, I didn't know what to expect or if I'd be allowed to pass.

With anxious faces, spectators dressed in robes and slippers lined the opposite side of the street, gawking and pointing. Orange security cones forced traffic into the far left lane. My car crept along behind a line of drivers craning their necks to see the fire. Flames leaped into the sky, and when I finally got a glimpse of the mansion, I sank hopelessly into my seat.

Roger! Where is Roger?

An ambulance screamed its way up the road behind me. I pulled onto a side street, parked, and glanced over the many vehicles in the driveway. Finally, I spotted Roger's Prius parked on the lawn behind the fence, out of the way of the emergency vehicles. But where was Roger? The gates stood wide open. I saw Grace talking with a police officer, but I couldn't see Roger anywhere.

The sight was horrendous, with flames engulfing the entire house. Where was Roger? *Heavenly Father, please save him!* I leaned my forehead on the steering wheel and prayed. I was a sinner for loving a married man. Even though I hadn't known he was married when I fell for him, I hadn't yet overcome my feelings for him. How could I lie to Heavenly Father when He knew my heart? *Please,* I prayed, *save Roger and Winnie, and I promise to go far away and never see Roger again. Please save his life!*

That was the hardest promise I ever made. I looked back at Emily sleeping in my back seat, totally unaware of her parents' danger. How could I keep my promise to always be there for her, and at the same time, keep the vow I just made to God?

Leaving Emily and Flo, I locked the car and crossed the street, keeping my car in sight and hoping the two would stay asleep. Grace, still dressed in pajamas, came running toward me. Her swollen eyes and tear-streaked face didn't give me any hope.

"He's in there!" Grace screamed.

"Who, Roger? What happened?" I feared the worst.

"A fire in Winnie's room! Roger went in. He went in to save her, and I haven't seen him come out." Grace sobbed aloud. I put my arms around her and she buried her face in my shoulder.

The sound of the flames, the heat waves mingling with the cold breeze, Roger gone—it all seemed like a nightmare. I glanced back at my car. All was still.

"Were you in the house, Grace?"

"Yes. I sleep in the room next to Winnie's, and the smoke woke me up. I tried to find her, but the room was in flames. I called 911, then Roger and the caseworker. I'm so sorry I couldn't save her! As upset as she was this evening, I shouldn't have left her alone."

Grace resumed her sobbing, and I kept my arm around her. Horrified, we stood helplessly watching the flames. Roger was in that inferno! I prayed aloud, "Heavenly Father, please save him!" I muttered the words over and over.

"My car is in the garage," Grace lamented, "and it's probably destroyed by now."

"I'm so sorry," I said, still holding to her. "Don't worry about how you'll get home, Grace. I'll take you. My car is across the street." Turning, I pointed to my SUV on the corner. "You can wait there. Emily is asleep on the back seat."

Grace started toward the vehicle. I pulled the remote from my pocket, ready to unlock the door, but then she stopped. "I see the caseworker," she called, pointing to a woman in the crowd. "I called her to let her know what happened. I need to talk to her." Grace hurried across the street.

I went to the sidewalk and peered through the fence and foliage. Several paramedics worked on a person on a stretcher, but I couldn't see who it was. When they began wheeling the gurney down the driveway, it was as if I was pulled toward it.

I had to know if the patient was Roger.

"Miss! Stop!" an officer yelled as I passed. Ignoring the order, I kept up my pace.

He caught my arm. "You can't be here."

"But—" I was so close. I shouted, "Roger!"

"Sorry, Miss. Go back across the street."

I have never in my life been mad enough to kick a policeman, but at that moment, I came close. "But I'm—I'm part of the family! I have their child in my car." I whirled to look into the policeman's face and was relieved to see Officer Ward. "Is it Roger?"

"Yes, and he's hurt badly. A beam fell on him."

I tugged without success to free my arm, then screamed, "Let me see him!"

The policeman hesitated but kept hold of my arm. "We're taking Mr. Wentworth to Banner Gateway Hospital."

"And Winnie? His wife?"

He let go of my arm. "She didn't make it. I'm sorry." He pointed to a gurney near the trees—a gurney that held a body covered with a white sheet.

Winnie! Poor Winnie! I thought. *What she must have suffered!* Then another thought came to me. *Maybe this is Heavenly Father's mercy—His way of releasing a crazy woman from her torment.*

The officer allowed me to go to Roger. When I put my hand on a tall paramedic's arm, he looked down at me and stepped aside. Roger's eyes were closed. His neck was burned, most of his hair was singed off, and soot covered his face. I stepped closer, trying to control my emotions.

In spite of his blackened face, he still looked beautiful to me. "Hello, Roger."

He opened his eyes and tried to smile. "Hello, Janie."

"Don't speak," I said, leaning closer to him. "Emily is safe. Don't worry about her. I'll keep her with me."

"Thanks," he whispered, then squeezed his eyes shut as if in pain. A tear rolled down his blackened face, leaving a path of red skin. "Winnie is dead. She's dead!"

"I'm sorry, Roger. So sorry." Tears filled my eyes. In a blur, I watched the paramedics roll the gurney toward the ambulance and lift it into the vehicle.

THIRTY

"I sometimes have a queer feeling with regard to you . . . it is as if I had a string somewhere under my left ribs, tightly and inextricably knotted to a similar string situated in the corresponding quarter of your little frame. And if . . . two hundred miles or so of land come broad between us, I am afraid that cord of communion will be snapt; and then I've a nervous notion I should take to bleeding inwardly. As for you—you'd forget me."

Janie?"

I turned around and saw Willa, wearing a shirt with the ambulance company insignia.

"Willa! What are you doing here?"

"I got permission to ride in the ambulance tonight. I told you I wanted to, but this is a lot more than I expected." She motioned toward the still-open doors of the ambulance and pursed her lips in concern.

"Roger Wentworth is in there," I said.

"I know. I'm so sorry." Her eyes became misty. "I wish it weren't him. I wish—"

I put my arm around her. "Please take good care of him. Tell your friend to drive safely." My voice quivered.

She nodded, and together we watched the medics secure the gurney.

"I'm so sorry all this has happened," Willa said. "It had to be Roger on my first ride. This is awful."

I wiped my tears with the back of my hand. "Call me from the hospital, Willa. Promise me you will. I want to know how Roger is."

She agreed as the last paramedic came running down the driveway. "Let's go!" he shouted to Willa. He shoved some medical bags into the back of the van and then closed the doors. Willa climbed into the cab.

When the ambulance left the driveway, I stood crying in the street next to a humming fire truck, watching until the ambulance drove far down the road and out of sight.

Officer Ward came to me and pulled a notepad from his pocket. "Do you know who of Roger's family we should notify?"

I knew he had a brother, but I didn't even know his name. "His mother is Margaret Wentworth."

"Do you have her number?"

I pulled the cell phone from my jeans pocket, found the number I had recently entered, and read it to the officer.

"I'll notify her right away," he said.

I scanned the crowd for Grace. She found me first and walked over to where I stood with the officer. "Emily is still asleep," she said. "At least someone is getting rest tonight."

"Chief!" A firefighter came down the driveway carrying a small, charred box. "This is what she used to start the fire."

She?

He held it out with a gloved hand for the fire chief to see. "There was a whole pile of them in the back bedroom."

Even from several feet away, I could see the unburned part of the Chocolate Art Forever logo on the box. My head began to swim.

Grace stared at the box with wide eyes. "She saved every one of the rose boxes and piled them in her room. By bedtime, she had worked herself into a tizzy, mumbling under her breath about you and Roger and Emily. Her obsessive thoughts drove her mad. I gave her some medicine but it didn't calm her down, and I tried to assure her that her fears about you weren't true, but she wouldn't listen to reason."

I couldn't believe it. Me, Miss Wallflower who hardly ever went on a date, a home wrecker? I had never meant any of this to happen. *Winnie, oh, Winnie! Forgive me for unwittingly driving you to the dark corners of your mind.*

Seeing the officer write Grace's statement on a notepad frightened me.

"Grace," he said. "I may be calling you for an official statement. Please give me a phone number where I can reach you."

Grace dictated her phone number. Then Officer Ward asked for mine.

"I didn't do anything intentionally to cause this," I told him through tears. "It was all so unfortunate the way it all happened. Please believe me."

"I believe you. I just need your information in case we need to investigate further." I stared at him a long time, hoping for reassurance. "Don't worry, no one will blame you for what has happened," he said gently. "This isn't the first time we've come here on a fire run."

Not the first time? I looked into Grace's weary eyes. She nodded her head, confirming the officer's words. She held my arm as we weaved our way across the street through the maze of police and emergency vehicles.

When we reached my SUV, Emily still slept soundly on the back seat, while Flo slept in the cargo area. In the glow of the streetlight, Grace looked exhausted. She turned one last time to look at the house.

"I hope we wake up in the morning and find this was all a bad dream," Grace said. She moaned as she sadly shook her head.

I pulled myself together so I could drive. I took the car key from my pocket as a policeman walked past us. That's when I noticed several officers scrutinizing the spectators. Assuming they were merely doing crowd control, I glanced over the crowd.

A woman wearing a floppy hat caught my eye. Though the hat partially hid her face, the sight of her stringy blonde hair made my stomach turn. The man standing next to her looked familiar as well. His long-sleeved sweater hid the tattoos on his arms, but I knew without a doubt who he was. They must not have seen me when I stood across the street talking with Officer Ward, or when I watched Roger taken away in the ambulance. They didn't see because they were hiding, huddled together and watching the fire from behind a fire truck.

I turned my back. "Grace!" I pulled her out of sight behind a block wall and tried to keep my voice low. "See those two standing down the street—the couple? The woman has long blonde hair and she's wearing a black sweater and a tan weaved hat."

Grace looked around the corner. "You mean Jennifer White? She's Winnie's caseworker. I called her after the fire broke out. On her orientation visit, she asked me to call her whenever anything happened to Winnie."

"Oh, Grace!" I moaned. "Did you tell her about the luau too?"

"Of course. What's wrong?"

It all fit together now. "That woman is no caseworker. She's a criminal, and the man with her is wanted for murder—the murder Winnie witnessed."

Grace's face went white. "And I called her about everything. I told her details! What should we do now?"

I peeked around the corner and saw Officer Ward standing in the street. He had also been on duty the night of the kidnapping, so I was sure he knew about Roger's case. "Go over to that cop and discreetly tell him those two are the suspects in the Wentworth case."

"I'm too scared!"

"If I go out there, the couple will see me, and they'll probably run. They'd never expect you to turn them into the police."

"Well—" Grace looked frightened. I urged her on, and she took a few voluntary steps but glanced back toward me. When she stepped into the street, the officer came directly to her.

"Miss, you have to stay on the sidewalk!" He took her arm and escorted her out of the street.

Grace kept her back to the crowd and spoke quietly to the officer. I saw him glance toward me. Pointing toward the crowd, I nodded. The officer left Grace and walked down the street towards Mike and Malinda, stopping to speak to another police officer.

I watched Mike spot the two officers. When the second officer put a walkie-talkie to his ear, Mike took a step backward, then another. He obviously knew something was up. I stepped out of my hiding place, ready to follow when he tried to get away. I started toward him and wanted to scream orders to the officers, for they seemed oblivious to what was happening.

In seconds, Mike was off in a run. "Get him!" I yelled in frustration, and the second officer took off running after Mike.

"Stop!" The officer hollered. "Detain that man!" At least three more officers heard the order and chased after Mike.

Malinda reached into her purse.

Bang! A bullet whizzed past my head. I dropped to the blacktop as the confused crowd scattered, looking for cover behind fire trucks and down side streets.

The first officer grabbed Malinda's wrist, sending her pistol skidding across the road. She screamed obscenities as she struggled to escape.

Even from a distance, I could see Mike pull out his pistol as the officers overtook him. "He has a gun!" I yelled, not knowing if anyone heard me, but a hand grabbed Mike's wrist, forcing the gun's aim skyward as it went off.

I turned to make sure a curly blonde head wasn't peeking out the window of my SUV. Flo raised her head and whimpered. I kept low, still shaking from Malinda's near miss, and went to my car. I heard another whimper from behind the car, walked around it, and found Grace huddled there.

"Are you all right?" I asked.

"Yes." She cried softly and visibly shook while hugging her knees to her chest.

"The police have them both now. It is safe to come out."

Grace sobbed again. "Winnie is dead. I shouldn't have left her alone."

I took her arm. "You can't blame yourself, Grace. You didn't know. Come, let me take you home," I said as I helped her to her feet, then unlocked the door to the front seat and helped her in. Then we listened and watched. Malinda now wore handcuffs and stood next to a police car. Mike was handcuffed too, and the officers brought him to stand with Malinda.

"These handcuffs are too tight!" Mike grumbled.

The officer opened the car door. "Don't worry. They're tight because they're new. They'll stretch out after you wear them a while."

It was a hard thing to do—to turn the key in the ignition and drive away from the mansion. I felt numb, as if none of what had happened was real, and I wished, as Grace had, that I would wake up to find it had only been a nightmare.

I drove the nurse to her home. "Will you be all right?" I asked.

She nodded. "My sister lives with me, so I won't be alone." She shuddered again, then put her hand on the car door. "Thank you, Janie, for coming. You've been such a support to me—to Roger, too, I suppose."

"About those accusations—there isn't anything between Roger and me. Please believe me."

Grace nodded. "Winnie wasn't well, as you are aware, but I know Roger was true to her. He is a good man. I tried to convince Winnie of that, but she wouldn't listen. I had no idea she would" —she stopped and frowned— "go so far with her phobia. Don't let yourself take the blame for any of this." She opened the door and got out of my SUV.

"Thank you," I managed to utter despite the emotion tightening my throat. "And thank you for taking care of Winnie."

Grace nodded and closed the door. I waited until she was safely inside her house. Then I put Flo in the front passenger seat to be a friendly face beside me in my time of grief.

I glanced at Emily sleeping on the back seat. Since the police had Mike and Malinda in custody, I could take her to my cottage. With a sense of freedom, I turned the car toward home.

By now, Roger would be at the hospital, receiving treatment for his burns. I wished I could have gone with him in the ambulance. I would have stayed and held his hand to give him support, but it didn't seem appropriate under the circumstances. Hopefully, someone who cared about him was with him. Maybe the police had reached his mother. As much as she disapproved of me, I needed to let her know Emily was safe and at my house.

I let the phone ring until the voicemail picked up. "Hello, Mrs. Wentworth," I said in my most professional voice. "This is Roger's neighbor, Janie Whitaker. I assume you have gone to the hospital to be with him. I just wanted you to know Emily is safe and with me at my place." I left my phone number.

Shortly, Willa called from the hospital to say they made it there safely. "Roger has third-degree burns on his neck and arms, and a broken leg and foot."

"May I come? Will they let me see him?"

"No, I'm sorry," Willa said. "They've taken him into the intensive care burn unit, and only family is admitted. His burns are pretty bad. Let's pray he makes it through the night."

THIRTY-ONE

"If you knew it, you are peculiarly situated: very near happiness; yes, within reach of it. The materials are all prepared; there only wants a movement to combine them. Chance laid them somewhat apart; let them be once approached and bliss results."

The sun created a dim glow in the eastern sky as I carried Emily into my apartment and laid her on the couch. After covering her with a blanket, I went to my room, knelt by the bed, and uttered an earnest prayer for Roger's life and for Emily's happiness. With Roger injured and in recovery, who would take care of the little girl? Her grandmother? What chance would I have to see Emily again?

My bed welcomed me and I fell asleep immediately. In my dreams, I heard Emily talking and giggling. I opened my eyes to see her through the doorway, sitting with Flo on the living room floor.

"Good morning!" Emily said when she saw I was awake. The two bounced into the bedroom and onto the bed. "I woked up in your house!"

I smiled, then moaned as I remembered the events of the night. "Shall we have breakfast?"

"Yes!" Emily said. "Flo is hungry too. I already fed her a banana."

I pulled myself out of bed and staggered into the kitchen. There, mutilated on a chair, was the banana. As I tore off a paper towel with the intentions to clean it up, the phone rang.

"Why aren't you at the shop yet?" It was Kylee.

Kylee! I glanced at the clock. It read 9:30 AM. Explaining the night's events in front of Emily didn't seem like a good idea, so I opened the front door. "Flo needs some exercise. Will you take her outside while I get us some breakfast?" The two happily ran into the courtyard, and I left the door open to keep an eye on them.

"You have Emily there?"

Kylee listened and expressed her sympathy while I explained about the fire and how I had crashed on the bed when I arrived home. Then I apologized for not coming to the shop on time. I left out the fact that Winnie was dead, for fear of what Kylee would say. I didn't want to hear it, not after the promise I had made to God.

"Then I don't blame you for not being here. Carmen and I can handle the shop. You get some rest."

Grateful for Kylee's support, I took a few cereal boxes down from the top of the fridge—the only place out of Flo's reach—and called Emily to come into the house. She left the door open, but I didn't mind the fresh air, and we sat down to eat. Emily and I chose Cocoa Puffs—hey, if it ain't chocolate, it ain't breakfast—and Flo chose three pounds of her usual monster feed.

A shadow crossed the door. Flo growled. I instinctively grabbed her collar and straddled her, then looked up to see

Roger's mother standing in the doorway, her face grim. "Hello, Janie. I see you've managed to be in the middle of my family again." Fire kindled in her eyes, echoing the red blouse she wore over a pair of black slacks.

Flo growled again. Not letting go of her collar, I stood. "Good morning, Mrs. Wentworth." I tried to sound cheerful.

"Grandma!" Emily squealed, spilling the cereal when she dropped the spoon. She flew into the woman's arms.

Mrs. Wentworth knelt to receive the child. They hugged for several seconds as Mrs. Wentworth buried her face in the curly locks. Seeing Emily with the woman, Flo calmed a bit.

Mrs. Wentworth stood, anger flashing in her wet eyes. "I blame you personally for what has happened to my son, and for Winnie's death."

Me? I glanced at Emily, who looked at me with questioning eyes. "How is Roger doing?" I asked her grandmother.

"He is at death's door." She didn't try to control her voice. "If you hadn't chased my Roger—"

"I promise, I never chased him. I—"

"—then Winnie wouldn't have lost her mind and set the fire. It's entirely your fault." She screamed, "Everything!" She bit her lower lip as her eyes filled and tears ran down her face.

"Mrs. Wentworth! Please, be reasonable, I never—"

"Never? I saw you two together, twice. I saw you in his arms. Can you explain?"

"I can. I was very upset. He only wanted to comfort—"

"Stay away from Roger, from Emily, from all of my family. Just because Winnie is gone doesn't mean you can have Roger now. If you ever come near any of us again, I will sue you. You are nothing but trouble!" The woman picked up Emily, then whirled and hurried toward her car on the street.

Flo went to the doorway and barked as I sank onto the

couch. After the trauma of the previous night, I couldn't handle Roger's mother's accusations. I started to cry. At first it was quiet whimpers, then sobs, and then full-out wails. Flo quit her woofing and started howling too. I'm sure we were a sight to behold, but I didn't care. I was a little girl again, crying in distress. The awful pain in my chest just had to be my heart breaking.

After I quit crying, Flo quit howling. I sighed, she sighed. I sniffled, she sniffled. Talk about best girlfriends sharing sorrows! She put her head in my lap and together, we sat in a slump.

We had been shafted.

This whole tragedy had ended in a way I could have never imagined. Guilt flared within me. I managed to keep Flo's head on my lap as I lay down on the throw pillow beside me.

"Please take care of Emily," I pled to the woman who had just fled my cottage, holding the precious little girl in her arms. Emily's delightful giggle echoed in my thoughts. Memories of Roger, Emily, Flo, and me together, ran through my mind—his smile, his touch, his voice. Out of habit, I attempted to turn my thoughts away from him.

The realization hit me hard. *But I can think of him!* He was no longer married, at least by civil law, so I didn't have to divert my thoughts away from him. Though I grieved for the death of Winnie, I could love Roger, and his mother's resentment toward me wouldn't change my feelings.

But one factor still held me bound. I had to keep my promise to Heavenly Father.

THIRTY-TWO

"Sir," I answered, "a wanderer's repose or a sinner's reformation should never depend on a fellow-creature. Men and women die; philosophers falter in their wisdom, and Christians in goodness: if any one you know has suffered and erred, let him look higher than his equals for strength to amend, and solace to heal."

So, that's my story about Roger Wentworth. Eight months passed since the fateful night of the fire. I went back to work the day after, and the next, and the next, as you do when exhaustion forces you to put one foot in front of the other. Life became routine again.

I didn't wake up in the mornings with the same enthusiasm. I went to church with a more humble spirit, not even caring if anyone gossiped about me.

As the cacao bean must go through a complex process to become refined, my spirit had been roasted, cracked, winnowed, and pulverized. I put my trust in the Lord and yielded to His will, hoping that someday my spirit would be refined.

Flo changed as well. She often stretched out on the floor and sighed. Sometimes we skipped our evening walk around the temple. Imagine that! And when we did walk, I often dragged Flo. That was a switch.

Against the wishes of the Wentworth family matriarch, I sent a get-well card to Roger at the hospital. He didn't respond to the card, but I couldn't keep myself from driving past the hospital and wondering about him.

After the fire, no one dared speak of Roger in the shop, which seemed so unnatural since he was our number-one topic for so long. Kylee and I had discussed the Roger ordeal thoroughly, so I'm sure she told the others not to talk of him around me.

Some days I'd fall into a slump, overcome with remorse, and want to hide in the kitchen. Then I'd say to myself, "I will get through this," and put on a smile and a cheerful act for customers.

Roger's brother and a friend moved Roger's and Emily's things out of the Taylor Palms apartment. Honoring their mother's wishes that I stay away from her family, I refrained from offering to help. I even kept Flo under lock so she couldn't be blamed for any mishaps. She would have caused several, I'm sure, hoping Emily had come back.

A family history addict named Olivia Hansen moved into apartment number 2. She and Sister Carter travel back and forth between family history libraries together.

I bought a wonderful house with a large, fenced yard. When I first walked through the door of the home, I heard it say, "Please buy me!" So I did.

Don't get me wrong—I still love the temple, but Taylor Palms wasn't the same as it used to be, and I needed new surroundings. Every time I saw Roger's old apartment, and every time Flo played in the courtyard, it brought back too many memories.

While my life revolved entirely around the shop again, I thought of Roger Wentworth often. In fact, no day went by that his gorgeous face, kind words, and soothing touch didn't flash through my memory. I missed him! Every day, I prayed for his complete recovery and that someday I might see him again. But I wouldn't go back on my promise to Heavenly Father, so if I saw Roger again it would have to be His doing.

Linc is like a sponge when it comes to learning about gospel principles. Jackie received her call and is now serving in the Washington DC North Mission. Linc finished his bachelor's degree at ASU, got a great score on the LSAT, and is now in law school. He still worries that when Jackie gets home, she'll be on such a spiritual high she won't want him anymore. Who wouldn't want adorable Linc? Kylee and I are determined to help him get ready to be married in the temple.

In the parlor hangs a new picture of the shop, painted by Willa. After the fire at the mansion, she took up watercolor painting to calm her soul. She's now dating her art instructor, a tall, skinny intellectual who is kind of wimpy compared to all the burly guys she has dated. But she likes him and that's what matters.

I discontinued our Signature rose. It had become Winnie's rose, and I couldn't see it without thinking of her and her tragic death. Then I'd think of Roger and how much I missed him and how we'd never be together again, and how we actually never *were* together. So rather than suffer daily, I retired the rose. Kylee and I held a sweet little service for it. She gave the eulogy and then I buried it. Yes, I wrapped the mold in a cacao bean bag, then put it into a Chocolate Art Forever box and hummed a funeral march all the way out to the dumpster. After tossing the box in, I dusted off my hands. That small therapeutic act renewed my spirit more than anything else I had tried. Silly, huh?

I like the new rose a lot better, so I named it after myself. It's called "Janie's rose." Like me, it is a bit short and squatty, not tall and elegant and delicate like Winnie was. The new rose is also heartier, meaning it doesn't break as easily and so yields better profits. In fact, I set aside all the molds that remind me of Roger or Emily—Alice, the laughing clown, and even the Great Dane—and put them on the top shelf of the cupboard to wait for another life. The only reminder I kept is Superdad. He is a daily attraction in the showcase and has sold very well. And while I changed the shape of his face so he looks less like Roger, he can't fool me. I still know.

With time, I knew I'd get over Roger Wentworth, just as I have every man I've ever been stuck on. Time heals all wounds, right? *Give me about two thousand years,* I figured, *and I'll be over him.*

Kylee's new OB/GYN claims to have found the cause of Kylee's infertility. We're all holding our breath to see what will come of it. My sister is back to her old bubbly self and is filled with new hope. (She says if she's blessed to have another baby and it's a girl, she'll name her Janie Rose.)

One Tuesday, I took my mail to the office to sort. Among the bills were two hand-addressed letters to me. I picked up the first and glanced at the return address. Wickenburg. In complete wonder, I pulled out the card, obviously a wedding announcement. There was a Post-it note over the photo that read, "Dear Santa Fe, Thanks for everything, and especially for saying no!"

I pulled off the sticker, and there, smiling happily, were Trevin Worliss and Tedi Campbell. It just goes to show that there is a Jill for every odd Jack out there. I taped the announcement to the wall under the price board for the whole world to see.

The next envelope had no return address. I opened it to find a card with multicolored flowers on the front, and read the impeccable handwriting:

Dear Janie,

I send my apologies for blaming you for Winnie's death. Roger has explained everything, and I realize now that Winnie was so ill that she turned all her madness toward you. Please forgive me for the heartache I must have caused you. I hope to be able to tell you these things in person someday.

Margaret Wentworth

I pressed the note to my heart and cried silently. What courage it must have taken for the woman to write such a note! Her simple, sincere words healed me in a way I'd never imagined. I put the card back in the envelope.

Even though she had forgiven me, the Lord had preserved Roger's life, and I had promised Him that if He did, I would stay away from Roger.

I glanced up at the clock: 8:58 AM. Although Tuesdays were now just like any other day, my stomach did a flip. I sighed. "Roger isn't coming back," I said quietly to myself, "so build a bridge and get over him."

Kylee was working in the front shop, wrestling with a roll of register-receipt paper that apparently had a mind of its own. For some inexplicable reason, I wanted to watch the door, so I stayed in the kitchen to start going through our autumn and Halloween molds. *We've come full circle,* I mused, *and so much has happened since last fall.*

The door chime rang.

"We'll be with you in a moment," I heard Kylee call. That is our signal that she is too busy and I should come quickly to wait on customers. I grabbed some logo boxes we needed in the front and carried them into the shop, then took another moment to put them under the counter. "There now," I said, standing. "How can I help you?"

I looked up into Roger Wentworth's face and a gasp caught in my throat. He looked different somehow, and his neck was scarred from the fire, but he was beautiful to me.

Tears sprang to my eyes. "Hello, Roger," I managed to whisper.

"Hello." He smiled his knockout smile.

Kylee scooped the supplies into her arms. "I'll—uh—" she stuttered and pointed toward the door "—I'll be in the office if you need me." What a dear sister.

"What do you have that's new?" Roger asked in his best businesslike voice. It felt like old times to hear him say that familiar phrase again.

"Uh . . ." I feared taking my eyes off him in case I'd awaken from this dream and he'd be gone. Unable to think clearly, I opened the case and slipped out the Superdad figure, forgetting I had given him one long ago, and placed it on the counter for him to see.

He looked up. "Very impressive, but it is for a woman—a very dear woman. And I'd like a card to go with it."

A woman! My heart sank to my knees as I took out the new chocolate rose and set it on the counter. Had he fallen in love with a pretty nurse who had nurtured him back to health?

"This is our new rose," I explained. "The woman whom our original rose had come to represent, passed away, so I retired it." I glanced up to see his reaction.

I knew he caught my meaning, though he waited another moment or two to speak. "She must have been very beautiful."

"She was. Very."

He looked at the new rose. "This one is even more beautiful, as is the girl I'm buying it for."

Now my heart crashed clear down to my toes. It was all I could do to remain professional and not bawl my eyes out. He had found someone to replace Winnie! Who was the lucky girl?

He added, "Will you wrap it? And I'd like to have it delivered."

"Of course." I took out a card. "Would you like to sign this?"

"Will you write the message for me?" he said, holding up a scarred hand.

My heart must have made it back into my chest, for seeing his hand caused a distinct pain where it had resided before the big crash a few seconds before. I wished I could hold the hand and kiss it and make all the hurt go away.

Instead, I picked up a pen. "What would you like to say?"

"Write, 'I'd like to take you to dinner this evening. Could we arrange it?'"

I wrote the message in my best writing, in spite of myself, and slipped the note into the envelope. "What is the address?"

"It's 485—" I wrote the numbers "—East Kimball, number 3."

I looked at the address. "But—" The blood drained from my head and I looked up. He only smiled and waited while tears burned behind my eyes. I let the pen slip from my fingers and could hardly speak, so I laughed. "That isn't fair."

"A dear friend once said to me, 'There is no better way to say I love you, than with chocolate.'"

"Roger, I—" A tear let loose and tumbled down my cheek.

He lifted the door at the end of the counter, then walked to where I stood and took my hand.

"I've done a lot of thinking while lying in the hospital and recuperating at my mother's. I miss Winnie, but the girl I married was gone long before the fire took her life, and now Winnie doesn't have to suffer anymore. I don't think she would have ever been well again."

"I'm so sorry."

He reached up and wiped a tear from my cheek. "I've thought so much about you, Janie, and the way you have loved my daughter, your kindness to Winnie, and the way you stood beside me through it all. I've thought of you every day since the fire. Please give me a chance. Let's start over. Nothing is keeping us apart now."

If I answered, I knew I would blubber, so I only nodded.

He pulled me closer to him. I looked into his eyes as he said, "Emily misses Flo so much. Let's try to make it work for her, too."

I laughed through my tears. "And for Flo."

"For Emily." He kissed my wet cheek. "For Flo." He then kissed my ear, sending tingles to my toes. "For you," he said, leaning down. His lips brushed mine. "And, especially, for me." Roger pulled me tight against him and lifted my chin. This kiss—sweet, wonderful, long-awaited—lingered, exactly like the first kiss I had imagined long ago.

The chime rang above the door, but for the moment, I didn't care to be professional.

Reader, I married him. A quiet wedding we had.

QUIZ

Here is the quiz I promised. Best wishes on a great score!

1. Roger Wentworth comes into the shop:
    A. Whenever he craves chocolate
    B. For Monday night FHE
    C. On Tuesdays at 9:00 AM
    D. To get away from criminals

2. Winnie Wentworth's profession is:
    A. Homemaker
    B. Psychologist
    C. Producer of the *Martha Stewart Show*
    D. Southwest artist

3. I live at:
    A. The LDS temple
    B. 485 East Kimball
    C. The chocolate shop
    D. In an apartment with a chihuahua

4. My dog, Florentine, is a:
   A. Chihuahua
   B. Overgrown poodle
   C. Great Dane
   D. Miniature horse

5. The name of our shop is:
   A. Chocolate Art Forever
   B. Chocolate Roses
   C. Tempe Sweets Shop
   D. The Chocolate Niche

6. Bjorn Enevoldsen is from:
   A. Bohemia
   B. Sweden
   C. Norway
   D. Denmark

7. Linc's full name is:
   A. John Art Linkletter
   B. John Lincoln Kennedy
   C. Lincoln Rockefeller Gates
   D. Linc Letter

8. The ward Christmas party theme is:
   A. Get kidnapped with Santa
   B. A children's nativity pageant
   C. Cancelled
   D. Christmas in Hawaii

9. Carmen's hobby is:
   A. Singing in the shower
   B. Hula dancing
   C. Ballet
   D. Picking up foreign men in dance halls
10. Cricket's medical problem is:
   A. Anxiety
   B. Acne
   C. Hiccups
   D. Plantar fasciitis

11. The name of the school Mike held Winnie hostage at is:
   A. Mesa LDS Institute
   B. Mesa High School
   C. Basketball Academy
   D. Mesa Junior High School

12. Sister Carter loves to:
   A. Babysit her twin great-grandsons
   B. Meddle in my life
   C. Spend all her time in family history research
   D. Bake chocolate-chip cookies for all the neighbors. Yum!

13. The criminals' names are:
   A. Jack, Malinda, and Mike
   B. Jo, Mike, and Jack
   C. Malinda, Mike, and Roger
   D. Mike, Jack, and Jill

14. My chocolate shop is located in:
    A. Tempe, Arizona
    B. Wickenburg, Arizona
    C. Salt Lake City, Utah
    D. Mesa, Arizona

15. Cricket is the daughter of
    A. Linc
    B. Kylee
    C. Carmen
    D. Tessa and Frank

16. Willa is:
    A. Daredevil
    B. Autistic
    C. Going on a mission
    D. Secret agent

17. Tessa and Frank are saving up to:
    A. Have a baby
    B. Invest in their own chocolate shop
    C. Buy a house
    D. Go on a cruise

18. Roger's profession is:
    A. An attorney for Eden's Garden
    B. An attorney for TriCorp Airlines
    C. Owner of Eden's Garden
    D. Chocolate entrepreneur

19. John got a job as a:
   A. Professional student
   B. Baptist missionary in India
   C. TV evangelist
   D. Janitor at Eden's Garden

20. Eden's Garden is a:
   A. Store that specializes in nuts
   B. Ladies lingerie shop
   C. Psychiatric hospital
   D. Plant nursery

21. Kylee's adorable children are:
   A. Paul, Whitney, and Jaxlynn
   B. Jim, Whitney, and Florentine
   C. Whitney, Paul, and John
   D. Whitney, Jill, and Roger

22. In this story, who proposes?
   A. Roger to me
   B. John and Trevin to me (separately, of course)
   C. Jim to Kylee
   D. Brother Toone to Sister Carter

23. Trevin's pet name for me is:
   A. Mahana you ugly
   B. Santa Fe
   C. Grandma Moses
   D. Wickenburg Beauty (I like it!)

24. My favorite book in high school was:
   A. *A Tale of Two Cities*
   B. *Riders of the Purple Sage*
   C. *Gone with The Wind*
   D. *Jane Eyre*

Answers: 1. C; 2. D; 3. B; 4. C; 5. A; 6. C; 7. C; 8. D; 9. B; 10. C, 11. D; 12. C; 13. A; 14. A; 15. C; 16, A; 17. D; 18. B; 19. B; 20. C; 21. A ; 22. B; 23. B; 24. D.

ABOUT THE AUTHOR

A third-generation Arizonan, Joan Sowards holds a bachelor's degree from Arizona State University. In addition to writing fiction, she composes music (see joansowards.com) and is a family history addict. She lives in Mesa with her husband and enjoys her five children, three grandchildren, Springer Spaniel, seven goldfish, and two hens.

Chocolate Roses is Joan's second novel. Her first novel, *Haunts Haven,* was published in 2009. She would love to hear from her readers and may be contacted at joansowards.blogspot. com.